the CRUX of the matter

Crisis, Tradition, and the Future of Churches of Christ

Jeff W. Childers
Douglas A. Foster
Jack R. Reese

The Crux of the Matter: Crisis, Tradition, and the Future of Churches of Christ

A·C·U
PRESS

ACU Box 29138
Abilene, TX 79699
www.acu.edu/acupress

Cover Design and Typesetting by Sarah Bales

Printed in the United States of America

ISBN 0-89112-035-1

Library of Congress Card Number: 00-109454

2,3,4,5

Table of Contents

Preface to the Series

From its beginning in 1906, Abilene Christian University has existed as an institution of higher education to serve the fellowship of the Churches of Christ. While we welcome students and supporters from a variety of Christian traditions who are sympathetic with our Christ-centered focus, we know who our primary constituents are. ACU's Bible Department, now the College of Biblical Studies, has for almost a century been a guiding light for our fellowship through its contributions in Christian scholarship and ministry. Thousands of missionaries, ministers, elders, teachers, and Christian servants have come under the positive influence of these godly professors. They have steadfastly upheld the Lordship of Christ, the authority of the Scriptures, and the necessity of living a life of Christian service through the church.

Abilene Christian University and its ACU Press launch the *Heart of the Restoration* series with this present volume. We pray it will help stimulate discussion and make a meaningful contribution to the fellowship of the Churches of Christ and beyond. Subsequent topics such as the nature and function of Scripture, the Church, worship, and Christology will follow. The authors are faculty members in ACU's College of Biblical Studies. In these volumes they will model a biblical spirit of unity in Christ, with individual perspectives on the details of the Gospel message. Above all, they are committed to the Lordship of Jesus Christ and to his church, and they are committed to restoring the spirit of the Christian faith "once for all delivered to the saints."

My special thanks go to Dr. Jack Reese who shared the dream of this series with me from the beginning. Dr. Doug Foster, as the editor of the series, has made the dream into a reality. My thanks go also to our benefactors who believed that the project would result in a clearer articulation of our faith and identity in Churches of Christ at the dawning of a new century. "Now to him who is able to do immeasurably more than all we ask or imagine, according to his power that is at work within us, to him be glory in the church and in Christ Jesus throughout all generations, for ever and ever! Amen."

–Royce Money

Introduction

We begin this project with a measure of apprehension. For one thing, in a book like this, it is likely we will be misunderstood or criticized. But criticism is not our main fear. Such is the risk of public ministry. Rather, our concerns are two.

First, with all our hearts we want to honor our heritage as children of Churches of Christ and uphold the values at the heart of this family of believers. All three of us can trace our spiritual ancestry in the Restoration Movement for generations.

Jack's grandfather's great-grandmother, in her words, "joined the Campbell Reformation" in the early 1840s. Her children migrated from Middle Tennessee to Pike County, Arkansas and helped establish a church in the little town of Corinth, which by the end of the Civil War, had became the largest Church of Christ west of the Mississippi. Her descendants, now spanning seven generations, have been active in Churches of Christ as church leaders, Bible School teachers, godly mothers and fathers, elders, and preachers, all committed to the ideals of restoration and the affairs of the Kingdom.

Doug's spiritual lineage in Churches of Christ includes at least five generations on both sides of his family. His great-grandfather preached throughout North Alabama and baptized hundreds of people, some still living and grateful for that godly influence. His grandfather was instrumental in establishing Mars Hill Bible School in Florence, Alabama in the 1940s, one of the first primary and secondary schools affiliated with Churches of Christ in the twentieth century. Doug attended Mars Hill for twelve years and Lipscomb University for four. His roots in and love for this heritage run deep.

Jeff's grandmother, strong-willed and insistent, urged her son's family to get involved in the small church on the West Coast that had become like extended family to her. The Childers' did get involved, serving faithfully in this congregation that eventually nurtured three generations of Childers faith. It was a non-Sunday School church. Jeff's long association with that wing of Churches of Christ, with its irenic leaders and strong sense of community, has been a blessing for him and his family.

Our main concern, however, is to honor God. It is a frightening thing to be engaged in public discourse for the Kingdom's sake–preaching, teaching, writing–presuming to speak on God's behalf. We approach these tasks soberly. We know we are imperfect in our understanding. We pray that we will say things that will strengthen the Kingdom. We hope we can point past ourselves to the sovereign God whom we claim as Lord.

Our use of the word *crux* in the title is quite conscious, of course. We mean it in at least three ways. First, to focus on the crux of any matter is to be concerned about the central issues, those things that are at the core. In Churches of Christ, it is time to rise above the pettiness that has sometimes marked our movement and to engage primary rather than peripheral issues. Some things are more important than others, and we want to focus on things that are most important.

Second, to be at the crux of things is to stand at a crossroads. Unquestionably, Churches of Christ face serious challenges in the opening years of the twenty-first century. Things could go in several directions depending on what we talk about and how we treat one another. We hope we can encourage healthy dialogue about the future direction of Churches of Christ.

Third, *crux* and its adjective, *crucial,* are the anglicized forms of the Latin root for "cross." It is here, ultimately, that we take our stand, not bogged down in issues of lesser concern, but testifying to what is at the heart of the matter: the crucifixion and resurrection of Christ. Such focus will help us avoid disputing over trivial things. It will cause us to place our doctrines and practices in appropriate relation to the center–to the heart of God in the person of Christ empowered by his Spirit. Moreover, putting the cross at the core will enable us to live more kindly and sacrificially. The future of our churches will depend on how our words and behavior reflect the cross of Christ.

More than that, our future ultimately rests not on our own shoulders but upon the work of God in our midst. We do not assume that merely understanding things better will make us better people. Transformation is the work of God. We believe he is involved in our churches, that he empowers and chastens us, and that he is moving us to greater love and service. Our most appropriate response to whatever crises we may be experiencing in our churches will be commitment to prayer and surrender to him.

The book begins by assessing current issues facing Churches of Christ. Chapters 1 and 2 describe the crisis of identity in this fellowship and several of its contemporary causes. Chapter 3 discusses the role of tradition, its importance in shaping our present identity, and the crucial role it must play in helping guide our future.

Chapters 4 and 5 look at the historical roots of Churches of Christ, providing background to our current issues and helping us see the religious and cultural stream in which are have been swimming. Chapter 6 describes other attempts to come to grips with the difficulties some of our churches are facing by surveying the contemporary literature of crisis.

Chapters 7 and 8 call us back to Scripture, to ways the Bible can be interpreted appropriately and practically, and to healthy teaching and pastoral ministry in our churches. Chapter 9 explores the message of 1 Corinthians and its call to focus on the crux of the matter. Finally, in chapter 10, we attempt to draw the strings together and provide a context for discussing the crisis, tradition, and future of Churches of Christ.

In general, this book is about attitudes and postures, about the big picture. It's not our purpose to suggest specific strategies and detailed answers. This is not to say that we are uninterested in being practical. On the contrary, we believe that understanding our cultural context, getting our tradition and history in focus, and appropriating a view of Scripture that is theologically-driven and cross-shaped are eminently practical. Seeing the Bible and ourselves in healthier perspective will have a huge payoff in our churches. But it is beyond our power to provide, in this volume, specific answers to every situation of congregational conflict. That is the place of local communities of faith under the oversight of godly leaders dealing with the unique circumstances of their situation. We want to suggest ways we can focus our conversations on the core issues that drive our faith and practice and which can transform both what we discuss and how we discuss it. Moreover, we want to equip leaders with ways of dealing with conflict and looking at Scripture that reflect the crux of the Christian faith.

These congregational leaders are the primary audience for this book. While conversations in academic circles about these issues are important, our purpose is to promote dialogue in our churches. In assessing our culture and history, we have made a number of generalizations. For example, the discussion of postmodernity in Chapter 2 and our Reformation roots in Chapter 4 do not reflect the complexity of the issues. A thorough examination of those periods would require far more nuancing than we provide. But these discussions provide a framework that will help us understand our circumstances at the beginning of the twenty-first century.

We have approached these critical issues with candor and care. We know we have not addressed all we could. We are aware that not everyone will agree, either with our assessment of the problem or the solutions we suggest. And we are open to those responses. Churches of Christ need more, not less, of these kinds of conversations–up front, out on the table.

It is not easy, as you can imagine, having three authors for a book such as this. We want to speak with one voice and write in a common style. This has not always been easy. We cannot imagine, however, working with people whom we love and respect more and with whom we have so much fun. We each have taken the lead in writing several chapters–Jack in chapters 1, 2, 9, and 10; Jeff in chapters 3, 7, and 8; and Doug in chapters 4, 5, and 6. However, we each have worked extensively in all the chapters and accept each of them as our joint responsibility.

We are indebted to Royce Money for challenging us with this project–not just this book but the entire *Heart of the Restoration* series. His vision is broadly reflected in this book. However, the views expressed are the sole responsibility of the authors.

We are also grateful for a group of colleagues who have been a part of this project since its beginning. Royce invited several ACU faculty to think with him about ways in which we could constructively participate in the dialogue among Churches of Christ. Our first retreat was at the Rose Mansion in Salado, Texas in May, 1998. From that time on, we have referred to this enterprise as the "Salado Project" even though several of the participants joined the team afterwards and have never visited that delightful town.

We appreciate the partnership of the Salado Group. Their ideas and encouragement have been invaluable, and many of them will have their voice in subsequent volumes in this series. These colleagues are Frederick Aquino, Ken Cukrowski, Randy Harris, Tom Milholland, Carroll Osburn, Tim Sensing, Eddie Sharp, Charles Siburt, James Thompson, Dwayne VanRheenen, David Wray, and Bill Young. We have gained many insights from each of these godly people.

Charme Robarts has served both as project assistant to the *Heart of the Restoration Series* and as an editor with ACU Press. More importantly, she has served in ministry in a variety of places through the years. Her insights, not only into the literary issues of this volume but especially in regard to Churches of Christ, have been especially helpful.

Finally, and most importantly, we are grateful to our wives. They have had to carry enormous loads, especially in the closing weeks of this project. Their sacrifices have been substantial. They have not just been supporters of this work. They are true partners in ministry and share with us our commitment to God and our appreciation of Churches of Christ. They, along with our children, have exhibited the spirit of Christ. We are grateful for their advice and their encouragement. To them–Linda, Linda, and Jeanene–this book is dedicated.

Chapter 1

Days of Confidence and Concern

The Cold War symbolized Americans' concern to have a safe nation in which to live, and the growth of churches and synagogues supplied a similar emphasis in spirituality. But the 1950s were to prove an exceptional decade, an ending as much as a beginning. The 1960s forcefully created the realization that things were not so easily controlled.

–Robert Wuthnow

A Golden Age

Many of us remember those days with a touch of nostalgia–at least those of us who are old enough to remember them at all. Those too young to have experienced them personally often think about them with a romantic longing, fueled by the collective memories of their parents or grandparents, and by the music that lives with us still. They are a part of our national consciousness now. The years after the Second World War. The Fifties.

They were confident years full of barely restrained and understandable pride. Our country emerged from the war brimming with optimism. No enemy could defeat us. No problem would impede us. If we could stamp out Hitler and bring the Axis powers to their knees in four years, in two hemispheres, if we could develop the technology to harness the atom and unleash its power at our will, if we could create television and rayon, jeeps, and synthetic rubber, then there was little we couldn't do if we put our minds to it.

So we produced. Automobiles, refrigerators, pre-fab houses, phonograph players, transistors, air conditioners, plastic, and countless new industries. And babies. Lots of babies. Little Boomers, many who would some day cause their parents no small amount of grief.

The G.I. bill allowed veterans to attend college in record numbers. Enrollment in the nation's colleges leaped in 1946 and subsequent years. The Boom was on! Jobs were abundant. The long Depression had finally been kicked in the teeth by the war effort. America had taken a seat at the head of the table of international affairs. At mid-century, it was the greatest superpower. Within a few decades, it was the only one.

These were the Eisenhower years. '56 T'birds. Interstate Highways. Bobby socks. Bobby Orr. The suburbs. *Leave it to Beaver.* Goldfish swallowing. "Say Hey" Willy Mays. Nickel Cokes. Elvis. Beehive hairdos. Stay-at-home moms. Roy Rogers. The '57 Chevy. *My Three Sons.* Dag Hammarskjöld. High school football. Audrey Hepburn. Dairy Queen. *The $64,000 Question.* Howdy Doody. 10-cent gasoline. Poodle skirts and saddle shoes. Motels. Motown. The Kingston Trio. Flattop haircuts. 45s. Blue jeans. Johnny Unitas. Pedal pushers. The Mickey Mouse Club. Ed Sullivan.

These were heady years. A time for confidence. A time to dream. A time to invest in the future–and in the present.

All was not rosy, of course. There were numerous countercurrents in the Fifties that would rise to the surface in the next decade–people and events of all political sentiments who disturbed the placid waters of this so-called Golden Age. McCarthyism rose and collapsed, exposing the arrogance of its mouthpiece as well as the gullibility of much of the populace. The Montgomery bus boycott awakened the national conscience to the underbelly of racism and hatred. The New Mexico desert hosted years of nuclear testing, not always to the health advantage of residents and federal troops. Hollywood moguls were blacklisted even if suspected of being only "pink" much less "red." Troops were sent to French Indo-China. Khrushchev found a new use for his shoe at the United Nations. The John Birch Society saw international conspiracy under every rock. Beatnicks became the caricature of an increasingly visible counterculture. Fidel Castro taunted American power. Poll taxes mocked universal suffrage. *Sputnik* rubbed American faces in the failures of our own rocket technology. No-fault divorce became the norm in several states. Little Rock schools violently resisted admitting black children to their classes.

Clearly, the Fifties had their troubles. But these unpleasantries were often pushed to the margins of the nation's consciousness, then and now. This was not a time to fret but to work for the nation's good. Not just work, but work hard. But also, especially for the children of the decade, it was time to have a little fun after the two previous difficult and serious decades from which we had emerged.

The Fifties, perhaps more than anything else, were a time to build–great cities, parks, highways, universities, computers, observatories, and ideas–things that were expected to last a long, long time.

Days of New Confidence

The present identity of Churches of Christ was formed in

significant ways during those years. What was true for the country was reflected in our churches–mostly for good, sometimes for ill. Our boys had served their country in exotic and faraway places, and upon returning immediately made plans to go back–to Germany, Italy, France, Japan, and, a few years later, Korea. A vision for "taking the world for Christ" began to ring in our pulpits. Our missionaries poured into Africa and South America, into all the continents, saving souls and establishing churches.

American Churches of Christ emerged from the Forties with a new confidence. Our preachers and elders were better educated, or at least they now had the means and incentive to become so. The newfound wealth of the American Fifties increased the budgets of the church as well. Businessmen (and in the Fifties they were almost all men) used their burgeoning incomes to support their own congregations. We began to emerge from our rural Southern roots to find our place in the cities, not just in Tennessee and Texas but even up North. We were moving to the "right side of the tracks" economically and socially, becoming part of the American mainstream. Some among us even received a measure of fame. Pat Boone was one of America's favorite entertainers. Lindy McDaniel pitched for the Cards. Ira North was praised publicly by Norman Vincent Peale. For many of us, there was a great sense of having arrived on the national scene.

The Fifties also witnessed a great building boom in Churches of Christ. Impressive edifices were constructed such as the Broadway church in Lubbock and its smaller architectural sister, the College church in Abilene, and West End in Nashville. J. M. Powell and Norvel Young reflected this large-minded and entrepreneurial spirit

UPI Says Church of Christ Fastest Growing Since 1950

DALLAS—The Churches of Christ are the fastest-growing major religious group in the United States, a new United Press International survey reveals.

From 1950 to 1965 membership increased by 135 per cent from 1,000,000 to 2,350,000.

The survey showed the Church of Jesus Christ of Latter-Day Saints (Mormon) grew by 61 per cent, making it the second fastest-growing major body.

Other fast-growing denominations listed by UPI were the Lutheran Church-Missouri Synod, 60 per cent; the American Lutheran Church, 58 per cent, and the Southern Baptist Convention, 58 per cent.

From the detailed study of growth rate statistics, the survey concluded the highest growth rates are found in the more conservative Protestant bodies which place a great emphasis on personal evangelism.

– Christian Chronicle, July 14, 1967

in their book, *The Church is Building.* Our buildings reflected our rising status. These were no storefront churches but great edifices that grew substantially, not only in size but in activity.

This was a time to re-think how we went about the business of doing church, and to crystallize the gains. We were especially interested in better educating our members. Innovations in children's education anticipated the next decade when Youth Directors would organize these same children, now adolescents, into youth programs. Education Directors provided Sunday School curricula to classes of young and old, lessons written by our own people at national publishing houses serving Churches of Christ. Education wings were added to our buildings, along with fellowship halls in a few "progressive" churches. Elders became more organized, and their meetings often began to reflect their experiences in the corporate world. Ministers were increasingly college trained. And Gospel preaching soared.

Giants walked among us it seemed, preachers of spiritual stature and eloquence, of power and energy. Every church held Gospel Meetings, often twice a year, sometimes two weeks at a time. We brought our neighbors and friends, some of whom were convinced of the error of their ways by the sheer logic and passion of the sermons. These were sermons uninhibited by the conventions of brevity we've grown accustomed to in more recent years. They were hard-hitting, bold, and urgent. Every point was punched with Bible verses. And there were many of them–both points and verses! The evangelist left no doubt as to what we were to do or how we were to live. Virtually every meeting led to baptisms, and congregational growth marked most years. "We're marching to Zion!" echoed triumphantly in our assemblies.

We'd never seen anything like it. Not in our life time, anyway. If this exuberance, this drive, this desire to build great churches had been known in earlier days in our history, we were unaware of it. But, then again, we knew little about what had occurred among us, or anywhere else in Christendom, before we were born. Nor did we much care.

Much of our fellowship's modern identity was forged during these years: creative programs, powerful preaching, worldwide missions, new and bigger buildings, higher social status, and, most importantly, a clear idea as to what constituted sound doctrine–what was right, and what was not.

Any family who traveled during those days would not have expected many surprises at whatever church they visited, whether in Brookline or Bakersfield, Rapid City or the Rio Grande Valley. If it were a "mainstream" church, its order of worship would be predictable. True, some congregations might have used a printed program, some would have been more inclined to sing gospel songs, university churches might have sung more "high church" songs, and the quality of the preaching might vary from place to place. But overall we knew what to expect. The boundaries of our public practices and doctrines were clearly set.

There were a few exceptions. We knew of churches not in the "mainstream"–churches with no Sunday School, churches in which worshippers drank from one cup in the Communion service, churches which didn't cooperate with one another because of doctrinal convictions. But each group kept to itself, mostly. Up North we might even run into some Churches of Christ that used a piano or organ, but we knew they weren't part of us. They really were Christian Churches, we figured, who had appropriated our name.

Of course, ethnic churches in the Fifties had some different practices from the predominately white ones. African American congregations did things a little differently, as did Hispanic churches. But there were few conversations among these essentially distinct communities. When we talked about "the brotherhood," we knew what that meant. When we spoke of "members of the church," we knew who was included and who was not.

We believed essentially the same things. We had the same name, were led by a plurality of elders, were served by deacons, employed preachers (or evangelists or ministers), worshipped *a cappella*, taught five simple steps to salvation including baptism (for the right reasons and by the right means), and observed the Lord's Supper every week. Women taught children, took care of food, and served quietly behind the scenes. We had no hand clapping, hand raising, or congregational kneeling (though some older members or the visiting evangelist sometimes knelt during the prayers). We did not recite the Lord's Prayer or participate in any congregational readings or have singing groups or solos. A single song leader led the worship, sometimes coordinating his songs with the sermon of the day. We believed in the Holy Spirit, and we knew he once acted with boldness and power, but many doubted that he did so any longer. We believed in Providence, though, and thought that God could work through the hands of the physicians who attended us. And we believed in the church. We worked hard to help our friends who worshipped in the denominations to understand the errors in their own practices and beliefs so that they might see the truth in ours.

This broad sketch may seem a caricature, but it is not meant to hide the fact that within this picture is a church of extraordinary vibrancy and virtue that transformed many lives, including two of the authors of this book who were born and raised in the Fifties. In this church was both passion and clarity. We owe our spiritual lives to what we were taught then. And we are grateful.

Growing Diversity in Changing Times

Many of today's youth in Churches of Christ will hardly recognize this congregation of the Fifties, not because there are no congregations that look like this any more–there are. Rather, the churches at the beginning of the twenty-first century reflect a diversity of practice hardly imagined forty years ago.

Within Churches of Christ today, one is likely to find contemporary music displayed with PowerPoint on overhead screens, worship teams consisting of both men and women, choruses and solos, congregational readings and recitations of the Lord's Prayer, hand raising and hand clapping, ministry teams, cell groups, elders who lay on hands and anoint with oil, and a few who have introduced instrumental worship. Some have women who serve the Lord's Supper, read Scripture, pray, or perhaps even preach in the assembly and teach classes for adults. Some congregations do not use the name "Church of Christ" on their marquee or letterhead, have members who believe that God will save at least some people who don't attend a Church of Christ, and believe the Holy Spirit is alive, active among us, and doing surprising and even miraculous things. And much, much, more.

For some, seeing such practices, which were inconceivable a few years ago, quickens the heart. It's what they've long been praying and working for much of their lives. For others, it's heart stopping. These innovations confirm their greatest fear.

How did we get here from there? How did the relatively predictable, orderly church of the Fifties evolve into a church of such diversity of practice and belief? And perhaps the greater question, who are we now?

Forty years ago, the answer to that question was clearer. We were the ones who had a biblical name, a biblical organization, and a biblical hermeneutic. We had the right understanding of salvation, worship, the Holy Spirit, the millennium, Bible classes, and church cooperation. We were the *New Testament Church.*

This assumption of "right understanding" of Scripture leading to the right practices and doctrines led some to argue, implicitly or explicitly, that other groups that did not believe or practice the things we did were not going to be saved. If we talked about how many Christians lived in New Zealand or France, we meant how many members of American-planted Churches of Christ lived there.

This view of ourselves in relation to other groups was a potent fuel for evangelism. If all others were lost, if we were the only ones who understood and practiced the Christian message rightly, then our task was clear. Evangelism, both at home and abroad, was propelled by a desire to help others get things right and, therefore, to become right with God. If every other group was going to hell, then everyone around us was a worthy object of our evangelistic zeal. In this climate, many congregations grew. Mission work became a large part of many congregational budgets. We certainly didn't struggle much with our identity–who we were, what we believed.

Beginning in the Sixties, and groaning under its own weight in the next two decades, the pillar of exclusivism began to crumble. This happened for at least three reasons.

First, more and more of our members felt uncomfortable with what was, at times, a rigid, judgmental, and even mean-spirited view of others. This attitude did not square with what we were reading in Scripture. Judgmentalism and legalism didn't seem to reflect the spirit of the New Testament, the character of Jesus, or the teaching of Paul.

Second, our study of Scripture began to call into question some of the conclusions we had reached in earlier decades. Still driven by our passion to be a back-to-the-Bible people, some began to scrutinize the doctrines and practices of our churches, and things weren't as clear as they had seemed just a few years before. We were sure of those things which were central to our faith, but some of the distinctive characteristics of our fellowship

Why Our Exclusivism Began to Crumble

- Many became uncomfortable with a judgmental spirit.
- Scripture called some of our beliefs into question.
- Increased contact with people in other groups forced us to re-evaluate our relationship with them.

began to be called into question–both by social influences and by fresh investigation of the Bible itself.

Third, as we began to move out of our isolation and have real dialogue and relationship with people from other religious groups, many of us were astonished to see demonstrations of the fruit of the Spirit in their lives. Some of *them* seemed to evidence more Christian virtues than many of *us*. How could this be if they had not come to the right understanding of the truth as we saw it?

For these reasons and others, the last three decades of the twentieth century in Churches of Christ witnessed more than a little self-reflection and even self-criticism. There was an increasing willingness to talk with others who were not part of our fellowship, and a desire to listen more. In looking at our own history, many began to discover a less judgmental heritage than what we had known in our life time.

All of this created an environment in which there was a loosening of the practices and concerns that marked the churches of the Fifties. This shift led to the diversity of the Sixties, which continues and increases for good and for ill, in the twenty-first century.

These developments did not occur in a vacuum, of course. Our own history has paralleled that of other groups and, in fact, our society as a whole. As the spirit of Churches of Christ was deeply affected by the national consciousness of the years just after World War II, so our churches have been shaped by the events of the last four decades of the twentieth century. We should not be surprised that the questioning of establishment views and values by the youth of the Sixties showed up in our churches during the same years. Nor should we be shocked that the decades of wealth in our suburban churches and the increased spending on our own programs and facilities along with decreased spending on world-wide missions and evangelism connects directly to the self-indulgent spirit of the last three decades in American society as a whole.

The question is not whether we will be influenced by our culture. We will be, as Christian communities always have. Rather, the question is how will we be a vital church, a biblically-rooted church, in the confusing and polarizing years of the twenty-first century? And, how will we resist those elements of our culture fundamentally at odds with biblical faith?

Our Predicament

In light of the developments within Churches of Christ over the last several years, many people in our congregations are choosing one of two different paths. On one hand, more and more of our children, and not a few of their parents, are leaving Churches of Christ and the values and practices of the Stone-Campbell heritage; a development that troubles us. Since many of us no longer believe that only members of Churches of Christ can be saved, exclusive loyalty to our own fellowship is in decline. With that, of course, comes the loss of some unique things that our churches have long stood for.

The three authors of this book are grateful for our heritage in Churches of Christ and unabashed about our commitment to it. We believe in its best instincts. We desire to go back to the Bible. We want to do Bible things in Bible ways, to participate in an undenominational vision of the church, to be Christians only but not the only Christians. We want our children to love these churches as we have. We believe Churches of Christ have something important to say to the larger Christian world. We mourn the loss of so many of our members who turn their backs on teachings we believe are central to the cause of Christ, such as baptism of believers by immersion for the forgiveness of sins and weekly observance of the Lord's Supper. Our desire to reaffirm what is best about the Stone-Campbell Movement stands at the heart of this book and this series.

On the other hand, we are repulsed by the spirit of exclusivism, legalism, and judgmentalism that still lives among us, and we question whether it has a truly biblical basis. We believe those who assume that *their* understanding of truth is *the* understanding, and who tolerate little if any diversity of teaching or practice, do not reflect the teachings of Scripture or the spirit of Christ. Perhaps more than any other factor, it is this exclusivist, judgmental spirit that has driven a wedge among our churches and fueled the polarization and divisiveness that has often characterized Churches of Christ in the twentieth century.

We have concerns about both paths. We reject the first because we are a part of a rich heritage with a unique and valuable understanding of Scripture, a commitment to its authority, and a high view of God's working through His people, the church. To jettison this noble heritage, we believe, is to lose something important, something of great value in God's Kingdom. We reject the second because it smacks of "another Gospel, which is no Gospel at all," as Paul describes the Judaizers in the opening verses of Galatians. The misappropriation of the teaching of Christ towards a kind of modern Pharisaism has two devastating effects. It undermines the teaching of Christ causing us, again in Paul's words, "to fall from grace,"–that is, to try to be saved by our own works rather than by God's gift to us. But just as important, it also means a greater likelihood that more and more of our people will choose the first path as they run headlong away from the second. It's both bad theology and bad practice. It's unhealthy and counter productive.

We should make one thing clear: We are not looking for a middle way. We are not suggesting that there are two hazardous ditches, one on each side and that we should avoid both just by choosing to stay in the broad middle. Being moderate, in and of itself, is no virtue. Choosing the middle ground is frequently just an excuse for not thinking. To do so is sometimes to be overly concerned with pleasing as many people as possible, rarely a good tactic when one is looking for truth. Often, it is the way of cowardice. We do not think Jesus chose the moderate way, nor did the writers of Scripture.

We are suggesting a third way, one that closely examines our own tradition and history so that we may not only see ourselves more clearly but also understand how our intellectual and cultural climate has affected how we use Scripture. For example, some among us assume that silence in Scripture is prohibitive–if it's not commanded in the Bible, we shouldn't do it. Others believe that such silence is permissive–if it's not condemned in the Bible, we have the freedom to do it. One position is called conservative, the other liberal. We believe both perspectives are flawed, both look at Scripture in ways that are inappropriate; both are substantially modern in approach and application. We are committed to exploring this more thoroughly.

The main thrust of the book can be stated succinctly. Many Churches of Christ are experiencing a crisis of identity fueled both by the decline of exclusivism and our growing diversity. Clues to our crisis and our future can be found in our past. Our history can help us see more clearly who we are today and how we got here.

Moreover, it can help us understand how we have looked at Scripture and how we can do so in an even healthier way. At the heart of the Bible is the story of God's mercy towards his undeserving people, culminating in the crucifixion and resurrection of Jesus. This is the *crux* of the matter, the place at which our actions and attitudes, our doctrines and practices must find their meaning. And, in these difficult days, it is the filter through which everything we say or do must pass. We not only want to call us back to Scripture but to engage in honest and constructive dialogue leading to appropriate Christian behavior, and to address difficult issues with an irenic spirit, all of which is in the best tradition of our own heritage. We invite you to join us on the journey.

Chapter 2

When Worlds Collide: The Church's Predicament in the Twenty-first Century

Things fall apart; the centre cannot hold;
Mere anarchy is loosed upon the world,
The blood-dimmed tide is loosed,
and everywhere
The ceremony of innocence is drowned;
The best lack all conviction, while the worst
Are full of passionate intensity.

–W.B. Yeats
"The Second Coming"

From the moment we arrived at Kimpo airport in Seoul we felt somewhat out of place. The scent of ginger and garlic sharply contrasted with the smell of antiseptic cleansers and fresh-brewed coffee more common in American terminals. Outside the airport, we could hardly escape the press of people, snaking through the maze of buildings, streets, and food stalls. This was certainly not downtown Abilene where it is rare for more than three people to occupy a sidewalk, even in the busiest of times.

Our gracious guides immediately took us to eat one of their favorite foods. It looked very much like a snow cone in a bowl, so we could hardly wait to try it. Shaved ice, fruit juice, a spoon full of powdered milk, and a smattering of jellied candy. And beneath the heaping mound? Surprise! A big scoop of black beans. We stirred our dishes valiantly and smiled.

> Two weeks in this marvelous country hardly removed our sense that we were strangers there. And even though the hospitality of our Christian friends was comforting, we still felt a sense of foreignness. Even in church, we never knew what would happen next. Because we couldn't understand the language, we were always a bit off-balance in the worship services. Sometimes the whole church would unexpectedly shout "Amen" and burst into exuberant audible prayer. Everyone. At top volume. We tried to join our brothers and sisters in prayer this way, mumbling aloud a few words of English, but it never felt quite natural to us. After a few minutes of fervent public prayer, the preacher would ring a bell at the pulpit. (We thought the bell was to announce when Sunday School was over. Little did we know.) At the sound of the bell, the noisy public prayers gradually subsided as the preacher summed up the petitions of the church and offered them to God. We had never prayed like this in America.
>
> We loved our time in Korea and returned two years later with our children. But we never lost the sense that we were disoriented.
>
> *–Jack*

Disoriented. What an interesting word. Medieval European builders, as they prepared to erect a great cathedral, made elaborate plans to lay out the foundation with the altar facing East–the Orient–towards Jerusalem. Before sun-up on the scheduled day, they drove a stake into the ground. The builder moved a few dozen paces away and placed an unusual instrument against the soil–something like a sewing needle re-scaled several feet high. Through the eye of the "needle," the builder peered, waiting for the dawn. As the sun began to peek above the horizon, the builder moved until he lined himself up with the sun and the stake in the ground. He *oriented* the foundation, laying a string due East toward the sun, marking one side of the structure. The building could not proceed until the structure had been oriented.

To be disoriented is to be confused as to which direction is East. It is to be off-balance, unsure of ourselves, unclear as to where we are going. What we used to count on to tell us where we are and what direction we're headed, now seems less clear, less accessible, or even absent. The church culture in many places has changed–sometimes slightly, sometimes momentously. Things are not what they used to be. Even in our own churches many of us don't always feel at home, almost like strangers in a foreign land.

This is no small matter. It's one thing to be faced with beans at the bottom of a snow cone. It's another to be disoriented about matters of significance, like how we worship, how we understand Scripture, how we obey God, how we go about the business of being the church.

Diversity is Disorienting

We used to know what "we all believed" in Churches of Christ. But now, some of our defining characteristics appear to be up for grabs. Who are we if we are not who we have always been? In every era there has been more diversity than we may have realized at the time, but the present days seem to hold special difficulties. For some, our identity is at stake, which is to say our focus, our future, our fellowship.

Some churches seem to be exploring the limits, doing things some people could never have imagined even a few years ago, trying to be faithful to their understanding of the call and will of God, or exercising what they see as their God-granted freedom. Others are becoming more deeply entrenched, drawing a line in the sand, declaring upon principle that they will not budge another step. Looking at Churches of Christ is like watching a rubber band being pulled and stretched more and more tautly. Can we tolerate this kind of diversity without breaking? Can we live together when our understandings and practices seem to be moving farther apart?

In times like these, as we have often witnessed in the past, our rhetoric can become tense, sometimes shrill, our behavior less than becoming. We hear stories of angry words, tart e-mails, inflammatory bulletin articles. Recently a preacher at a fairly progressive church innocently opened an electronic attachment sent by an upset church member in another part of the country. It was a Trojan horse. The virus it contained destroyed all his computer files and church records. One minister discovered one Sunday morning that over the weekend someone had cut the wires to the microphones of the worship team. One preacher refused even to sit down with his more conservative counterpart to engage in a mediated conversation for the purpose of reconciliation. Most communities can tell stories about churches that have recently split into two–or three.

But these are the extremes. More commonly, we just shake our heads in bafflement, or assume that over time these disagreements will work themselves out, or fold our hands in resignation. In this light, our future seems increasingly unclear.

Who is to blame for all this? Who is responsible for this widespread disorientation? Is it the "progressives" who seem to be pushing for change? Or are the "traditionalists" driving away those who disagree with them? Does the problem lie with certain preachers? Particular brotherhood magazines? Some of our Christian universities? Surely someone can find the culprits, explain what they are doing, and show them the right way. Or at least warn the rest of us to guard against the ideas and practices that are creating this menacing new climate. (Attempts to do just this have produced a growing assortment of books, some of which we will look at in Chapter 6.)

But we should recognize that changes like the ones we are experiencing–and many far more substantial–have occurred before. Perhaps the experiences of believers in times past can provide us a glimpse of the sun so that we might gain our bearings again, see which way is "East," and re-check our markings so we can go to work again, facing the future more confidently.

A Perspective From History

Imagine that thriving church in Jerusalem in the early days of the Christian movement. It had experienced extraordinary growth. Many faithful Jews from Judea and Galilee and throughout the Jewish diaspora had proclaimed Jesus of Nazareth as their Messiah. They met in homes and synagogues, being taught by the Apostles, serving one another, praying together, eating common meals, sharing their common possessions. But within a short time, not only had some ill-cultured Samaritans joined their ranks, a fact not a little disturbing, but also the new church in Antioch to the north had dispatched missionaries to Crete and Asia Minor. Now Gentiles were pouring into churches all over, bringing with them foreign customs and ideas. They had strange accents, wore strange clothes, and ate strange food. They had not known the ways of God, had not grown up with the stories of the patriarchs.

Even after the so-called Jerusalem conference, described in Acts 15, at which the Gentiles were publicly accepted into the fellowship, the tension between Jewish and Gentile Christians never seemed to go away. Almost every first-century church experienced problems. Each group looked down on the other as culturally or spiritually inferior. As the number of Gentiles in the churches grew, some Jewish Christians became more frustrated or discouraged. The legacy of this tension, and the effective growth of the church in spite of it, stand as a monument to God's faithfulness. But the disagreements had their consequences. Within a century, relatively few Jewish Christians remained. The Christian movement had become primarily a Gentile enterprise.

Imagine being a Christian in the Roman Empire of the early fourth century. Christianity was outlawed. Thousands had already been martyred for the Christian faith–witnesses to how far committed disciples would go to defend their God and their practices. They were harassed by officials, ostracized by society, shunned by their neighbors.

But when the community of saints gathered in their homes, the fellowship was special, all the more so because of the fear they faced every day and the frustrations of living in a world that had a difficult time understanding their beliefs and often pressured them to conform. The service was relatively simple. They read Scripture and encouraged one another to be faithful. They embraced one another as family, brothers and sisters in Christ. Betrayal would be disastrous. Huddled together in their modest houses, they offered their prayers, shared their bread and wine, and prepared to re-enter the hostile world where they worked and lived, fed and sustained by their community and their faith.

But the most amazing thing happened. Out of the blue, the emperor himself converted, or at least so it seemed, and the effects on the empire were profound. Constantine, as he was preparing for the battle that would determine the future ruler of the Roman world, declared his allegiance to Christ, and his armies won a sweeping victory. Then everything changed. In bits and spurts, to be sure, but in a very short time, the face and practices of Christianity changed.

Those simple times of worship were utterly transformed. As the church moved from ostracized sub-culture to the center of power itself, and as the leading officials of the empire proclaimed themselves believers in Christ, the practices of the church began to reflect the proceedings of the imperial courts. No longer did the Christians have to meet in their own homes. Roman officials now handed over certain municipal buildings and courthouses to the Christians. And soon new buildings were erected for the specific purpose of Christian worship, designed like the Roman structures that housed the offices of government and the temples of worship. Like the Roman courts, church began with a processional, with banners and incense, and a parade of worship leaders and dignitaries. The people, now in quite large numbers, congregated in the assembly hall as they were led and taught from places of authority at the front of the building by church officials quite distant from them. Times of worship were carefully scheduled, the increasingly elaborate worship practices carefully planned.

For the simple Christians who had remained faithful during the years of oppression, these developments were shocking. Church buildings? Pulpits? Communion bread resting on silver trays? Masses of people listening passively as church leaders performed their actions at the front of an auditorium? This was surely not what God intended. These dramatic changes produced a genuine crisis for many of the faithful, igniting controversy from Persia to North Africa.

Fast-forward eight centuries later. What began in the Western churches in the fourth century had fully flowered by the twelfth. The changes, many of them fairly recent, would be consolidated and made official at the beginning of the thirteenth century, at the fourth Lateran Council in 1215. Bishops, especially those practicing the Roman liturgy, wanted to make the elements of the Christian service holy. These elements shouldn't be common; they must be special. For this reason, musical instruments were introduced into the services. Elaborate musical presentations became the norm, replacing the simpler form of vocal music, which, had always been the practice of the church (and thus referred to as *a cappella,* "in the manner of the church"). Similarly, from the ninth century, the common bread, leavened bread, was replaced by unleavened bread. Using regular table bread had been the practice of the churches for centuries of Christian worship from very early days. Church officials introduced unleavened bread apparently because it would be considered special, set apart, holy. (Church leaders in the East accused the Western church of introducing Jewish practices, of becoming Judaizers because of this innovation; their descendents, the Eastern Orthodox, use leavened bread to this day.) Priests continued to expand the practice of wearing special clothing to separate themselves from the common people, the laity.

These changes, some of which had been evolving over centuries, were difficult for many to accept. As in every other period in the history of the Christian movement, there was strong dissension, polarization, vocal public exchange, and substantial internal political maneuverings.

Over time, of course, what were considered innovations became the regular practices of the church. When reformers advocated changes in these practices, they were vigorously opposed. For example, those who taught that the Bible should not be controlled by the priests but should be accessible to the people and translated into their own language met substantial resistance–John Wycliffe faced years of persecution; William Tyndale paid with his own life. Ironically, the Protestant Reformation, itself a rebuff to Roman Catholic orthodoxy, resisted the more radical reformation of the Anabaptists who opposed infant baptism and inaugurated a movement of independent, non-liturgical churches. Many died for their cause.

In early nineteenth-century America several church leaders, mostly Presbyterian, left their fellowships and challenged the denominalization of Christianity. They encountered strong opposition to what many people thought was a radical message. They called people to be "Christians only," "speaking where the Bible speaks and being silent where the Bible is silent." They suggested that even ordinary Christians could understand the simple message of Scripture and challenged churches to go "back to the Bible." Leaders like Alexander Campbell were accused of being divisive as they rejected the creeds of the church. Others reacted against what they thought was a dangerous spirit of Americanism as these leaders assumed all Christians in the pews could understand the message of the Bible without the need for clergy. It was perceived as a kind of democratizing of the church.

These events provide a backdrop for understanding our own circumstances at the beginning of the third millennium. In each instance, there were major shifts in the historical context in which these churches functioned. Their church life and practices were directly connected to major social changes. In each age, Christians had to make decisions about how they would live and what their churches would practice. They had to base these decisions upon their own experiences, their understanding of the will of God, their views of Scripture's teaching, and the intersection of Christian beliefs with the prevailing understandings of the times. And in each instance, there was dissension, disorientation, and unrest.

Thoroughly Modern America

Not surprisingly, we face similar circumstances. Our disputes and unrest are neither new nor unique to us. Every religious group in America is experiencing some kind of disorientation. Since the Second Vatican Council of 1963, Roman Catholics have been involved in sometimes heated discussions about liturgy, doctrine, and church authority. Most mainline Protestant denominations have seen major disputes concerning such issues as worship, the ordination of women, and whether to approve homosexual marriages. Evangelical churches have experienced polarization and even divisions over such things as worship styles and the nature of biblical authority. Impassioned discussions among leaders in the Southern Baptist Convention over such issues have generated scores of articles and books from all sides.

WORLDVIEW

People are talking a lot today about changing worldviews. A worldview is the overall perspective from which people see and understand things—the collection of beliefs and experiences that becomes the lens through which they perceive the world.

What is going on? Why so much unrest? Is it only coincidence that all of these groups, covering the entire theological spectrum, over a variety of issues, are facing such difficulties?

The answer lies largely in what has occurred in Western civilization and especially America over the last century. We are experiencing what many are calling a cataclysmic shift in the way people think and act. Some suggest that what we are going through as a culture is comparable to what occurred five hundred years ago in the Renaissance and Reformation. At such times, not just *what* people know but *how* they know undergoes substantial change. And we may be at the front of just such a cultural wave.

Of course, it's too early to tell. It may be a hundred years or more before anyone could say for sure what is occurring in our day. But all the signs point to a major transition in Western culture. Such a change is bound to affect the church, so understanding this transition could provide some clues as to how we should think about our current circumstances.

A number of people have divided the history of the Western world into three major epochs–*pre-modern*, *modern*, and *postmodern.* This is a simplistic classification, of course. The seeds of so-called modernity, for example, can be found as far back as ancient Greece at the height of what we are calling a pre-modern world. Our current age is actually a vigorous mixture of both modern and postmodern. By looking at these periods in a cursory way we cannot do justice to their complexity, but a brief description of the basic characteristics of each epoch will provide a helpful framework for our discussion.

The Pre-Modern World: Faith and Superstition

In the *pre-modern* world, generally up to the fifteenth or

sixteenth centuries, virtually everyone believed supernatural forces caused or influenced every human experience. Such things as disease, accidents, business failures, shipwrecks, miscarriages, crop yield, and rain were seen as the products of divine intervention rather than resulting from material causes. This belief left people vulnerable to superstition and fear.

For this reason, priests and religious leaders, whether Christian, Jewish, or pagan, wielded considerable power by virtue of their spiritual knowledge, which the people often saw as almost magical. For example, in the medieval church, priests administering the Eucharist would "elevate the host" or raise up the communion bread. People would bring their sick to gaze upon the bread hoping for a miracle. Witches stole bits of it to perform spells. Fear and superstition were the dark side of the prevailing belief in the supernatural.

A positive feature of the pre-modern world was the value of community. The "individualism" French philosopher Alexis de Toqueville found in early nineteenth-century America was not yet familiar in this pre-modern world. Community values, the importance of village hospitality, and the need to protect one another were common commitments in the pre-modern world.

Finally, for most people in a pre-modern world, truth was absolute; it could not be conceived as relative or mediated through the experience of the individual. Whatever the specifics, one's view of truth was all-pervasive and stood at the center of existence. Every religious tradition, and certainly the Jewish and Christian heritage, assumed ultimate and infinite truth. And this truth was embodied, Christians believed, in the person of Jesus.

The Modern World: A Triumph of Science and Reason

Between the fifteenth and sixteenth centuries a revolutionary cultural shift occurred that gave way to what we call the modern world. This time frame extends to the twentieth century. Old understandings and values underwent substantial changes for several reasons. As people increasingly understood the nature of the universe, they could explain many things by natural rather than supernatural causes. Advances in astronomy, maritime navigation, meteorology, physics, biology, psychology, and other sciences led to a shift of focus–toward physical rather than spiritual explanations of things, toward knowledge of data and the authority of science. Rain could be explained without reference to the divine. Physical illnesses were increasingly assumed to have physiological, not spiritual, causes.

These developments had several consequences. One, with the rise of scientific methods and assumptions, along with other philosophical and cultural shifts, the dominance and power of religious authorities declined. Religion was no longer the sole owner of truth. Knowledge was power, and education increased understanding and influence, helping fuel the decline of the dominance of the church in individual lives.

Two, in modernity the individual began to gain ascendancy over community. Single individuals could research, think, formulate, hypothesize, discover, synthesize, and inform without answering to institutional authority. Western societies became increasingly interested in individual rights and celebrated the power of individual minds.

Three, modernity is characterized by a growing belief in the inevitability of progress. Humans are learning more and more. We are understanding the origin and the make-up of the material world and devising ways to cope with our circumstances with more efficiency and greater benefits. The triumphs of modern medicine, physics, chemistry, and microbiology, the discoveries of the great explorers from Vasco de Gama and Amerigo Vespucci to the astronauts and cosmonauts of the last forty years, the life-changing inventions which we have come to take for granted, all have created the sense that the world is getting better and better.

Moderns have been marked by self-assurance, confidence in human ability, and considerable optimism. These characteristics, mixed in their effect, have had a substantial impact on how we think, how we view God and ourselves.

America was established upon these modern ideals and principles. Americans have no pre-modern past except through their cultural ancestors across the sea and the heritage, mostly forgotten, of the original inhabitants of this land. Ours has been a nation of extraordinary optimism, can-do spirit, pride in human achievement, the triumph of democracy, and the value of the individual. The dominant myths of America are that we can solve it, organize it, plan it, build it, and support it, whatever the "it" is, better than any other nation or culture in human history. At least for many Americans, that's their central story, their identity, their self-understanding. It is often the filter through which they see the world.

Yet it is this world, this modern world, that has shown gradual signs of deterioration throughout the twentieth century. And in the wake of its failures has emerged growing disorientation and despair. But if it has produced so much, if there have been so many benefits of this modern world, why is it in decline? How can we suggest that it has in some way failed? And how do these developments affect our current crisis in Churches of Christ?

Part of the answer is the profound confidence in human ability at the heart of modernity. We had become too secure in our own understanding. We took pride in our independence, but we had not always seen the downside of our resistance to depend on others, much less on God. As a society, we have demonstrated less need for him, more reliance on ourselves. And while Western civilization has accomplished much, and the discoveries and inventions have given us new glimpses of God and the world He created, it has also bred short sightedness, extreme competitiveness, and intolerance. In it were the intellectual seeds for modern atheism; and it has fueled what became in the last years of the twentieth century a full-blown consumerism.

Modernity assumed that physiological and rational causes could ultimately explain almost everything. For many, in such a world revelation, truth, virtue, ethics, and morality have become detached from their moorings. If what happens around us can be explained without reference to God, then God can largely be bracketed out of our conversations and concerns. In modernity, he is often seen as superfluous, quaint, or irrelevant. And the consequences of that are evident all around us.

COMING TO TERMS WITH OUR AGE

Pre-modern, modern, post-modern. The terms themselves show how difficult it is to get a handle on the societal shifts in Western culture. Even to try to do so is a "modern" thing, and the terminology reveals how much stock we put in modernity. The so-called "modern" may always be with us, but it will never look the same.

American optimism reached its zenith as the twentieth century dawned. But a number of things happened to chip away at its underlying modern assumptions. World War I, The War to End All Wars, was a shocking event.

Though called a "world war" it took place almost completely in the Western world, this modern world. Virtually all the players in this conflict saw themselves as Christians. The physical effects of the war were more devastating than the world had ever seen–mountains of bodies, the terror of the trenches, the horrors of chemical warfare. Western intellectuals never regained their footing completely. The optimism of the turn of the century took a devastating blow.

Too quickly came the Great Depression, the rise of Nazism, the Holocaust, and World War II, which was in large measure the unfinished business of the First World War. The twentieth century, supposedly the zenith of human progress, saw more bloodshed and witnessed more wars with greater devastation than any century in history. The myth of human progress took a severe beating.

The seeds of the demise of modernity emerged within its greatest product–science. The triumphs of Isaac Newton's understanding of the universe, with all its order, predictability, and benefits to human progress, suffered unexpectedly but markedly in the twentieth century. And it did so at the hands of his intellectual descendants.

Einstein's theories of relativity were a stunning correction to the Newtonian view of the universe. His discoveries of the interrelationship of matter and energy, and his supposition that even time was relative were a bombshell. But even this could not compare to the revelations of quantum theory. Even Einstein was aghast at what the quantum physicists were saying, and he argued against them much of his life, though most of the evidence is against him. Quantum theory cast serious doubt on the predictability of the universe, an assumption that is the foundation of almost all practical physics. Atoms apparently jump from one orbit to another without obvious cause. While the movement of particles could be predicted statistically, there is no identifiable cause, as if events, at least at the atomic level, were governed solely by chance. Perhaps, it was asserted, causality in the universe itself was merely an illusion.

Paradoxically, it was twentieth-century physicists who began to undermine agnosticism among scientists. For some physicists, at least, appreciating the limits of human understanding has brought a greater sense of humility and a growing view that some things are beyond our grasp and that God might be the author after all.

In the final analysis, modernity has lost some of its impetus in part because it has not lived up to its promise. The world, at least in the things that matter, does not seem a better place than it was before. In the twentieth century, humans may have come to learn more and work more efficiently, but they are not happier or more moral. Modernist optimism has given birth to cynicism and suspicion. We can split the atom but we cannot create belonging.

In the 1950s, many predicted that by the end of the century technical innovations would reduce the average weekly workload. But today many are more overworked, overstressed, and frantic than ever. High production levels are common. Healthy human relationships are not. Modernity, again and again, failed to live up to its promise.

This is not to assert that the engine of modernity and its effects are dead or its effects primarily negative. Scientific knowledge and technology will continue to grow. Human understanding will continue to increase. But it may be impossible to return to the naive optimism of a century ago. Too much has happened. We've seen the downside.

The Postmodern World: New Frontiers

The phenomenon of postmodernity has been growing throughout the last half of the twentieth century, though its roots extend to an earlier time. Its core characteristic is significant diversity, making it difficult to define. But whatever it is, it is a reaction to many of the impulses of modernity. It is less confident in reason, more inclined toward experience. It can be stridently individualistic, yet it also shows a tendency towards community. It is less optimistic and more suspicious, less idealistic and more pragmatic. It does not

REMEMBER WHEN...

Some will remember the TV commercials of the 1950s and 60s. In those days, companies convinced us to buy their products by listing facts and citing surveys, by putting experts on the air to dazzle us with scientific jargon.

Today things are different. TV commercials are sights and sounds, action and color, superstar personalities. Companies get us to try their product by connecting it somehow to an engaging story or an amusing plot which may have little or nothing to do with the product itself. As far as this generation is concerned, statistics and experts don't mean much.

Like it or not, the ways in which people in our society decide who to trust have changed.

Many can remember 25 years ago, or even less, when magazines were arranged in a rather linear way. The articles were straightforward, one after the other. You read one, then the next.

Today, magazine editors cram articles with boxes and quotes and interviews, choosing different fonts without any obvious sense of coordination (at least to a modern). On any given page, you can start almost anywhere—read a summary quote, look at a graph, browse a related story, smile at a cartoon. Why, even books these days seem to be filled with boxes and quotes, interrupting the narrative with definitions or related materials, or inviting readers to Remember When...

These non-linear approaches, with visual stimuli everywhere, and often with self-parody and irony, are typical of postmodernity. Those who were raised in a different age can find it exasperating. But it's a different day, and if history tells us anything, we're not likely to go back.

assume humans can know everything. It openly challenges those who think they've gotten it right–those who can understand it, name it, and explain it. It is prone to ambiguity, not certainty; human limitations not infinite human possibilities, cynicism not trust. It assumes a world largely unordered and unpredictable, more relative, less concrete.

The world of postmodernity is not necessarily a better world. Its cynicism and suspicion often work against Christian values. Its lack of order often stifles reason. This worldview is not likely to produce better readers or greater thinkers. On the other hand, postmoderns tend to be more open to spiritual possibilities, less reliant on human wisdom and accomplishment, and are often more pragmatic in their interests. Within postmodernity, many people are less likely to believe something because they've "always believed it." They are intolerant of intolerance. They are less interested in the head, more interested in the heart. It is not a better world, but it is different. And the effects of those differences are being felt widely in our churches.

In a postmodern world, allegiance to institutions loses much of its grip. Young believers in America are typically less loyal to their denomination or religious heritage. They often believe that denominational boundaries are rather arbitrary. They're not very interested in the accidents of history that created these distinct groups, but they are interested in truth wherever they find it and can be quite patient with people whose views are different from their own. They are not inclined much to debate. They rarely argue. But they will leave. They can smell a hypocrite a mile away. (Suspicion breeds this kind of discernment.) They will not be patient with church leaders who talk about discipleship but who do not live it, who insist on rules but are not concerned with justice.

The old rules of the game no longer apply. Those who are living by them may find themselves left out of the conversation or talking only to themselves. Children who have grown up in this new cultural context can hardly understand how Christianity can be reduced to a system, how issues that are never discussed in Scripture have emerged as requirements in some of our churches. And they will be impatient with the conversations about these matters.

They will not tolerate worship that has the right practices but not the right heart. And many of them will be willing to sacrifice things that some of us believe are of first importance, including baptism and the weekly observance of the Lord's Supper, in order to participate in worship that is meaningful and moving.

Obviously, our analysis is overdrawn. The general characteristics of a particular age may not apply to any specific individual. Those of us who grew up in a predominantly "modern" age are not likely to be more arrogant or less practical than our younger friends. Many in the younger, more postmodern, generation can read and think quite well; they will not necessarily see truth as relative. People from both worldviews can be optimistic or hypocritical, interested in justice as well as righteousness.

But with such cautions clearly in mind, we must not miss the point. A cultural shift in the West is occurring. It gives no evidence of being a passing fad. Its roots lie early in the twentieth century and its effects should be felt for generations to come. The impulses of modernity are not over, of course. They may never be. The gains and methods of science will not be lost in the coming centuries. But, there is considerable evidence that people are beginning to view knowledge and the world differently. These differences are real and the consequences significant.

Conclusion: Perils and Possibilities

This is a frightening situation for many of us, especially in the church. It's hard not to be both encouraged and concerned. As W. B. Yeats poetically expressed it early in the twentieth century, the coming of a new age always brings with it the feeling that "things fall apart; the centre cannot hold." Those of us who grew up in a time in which reason, order, systematic thinking, and the triumph of objective fact were of first importance find it difficult to understand and relate to many of the younger believers. But at the same time, their yearning for spiritual food, their desire for righteousness, and their willingness to serve others is impressive and inspiring.

So, it's a mixed bag. But one thing is for sure–we can't go back. We can't resurrect the Fifties. We are living now. And we must choose. We can try to couch things in the language of modernity–linear, systematic, discursive, rational–but we may find ourselves outside the conversation. We can accuse, argue, defend, and label, but when we do we will more than likely push ourselves to places of irrelevance. We can jettison our past to live in the present, but we will forfeit not just our heritage but our spiritual trajectory, our questions, our identity, our very soul. Or we can find a meaningful way to stand within history, appropriate the blessings of our heritage, use the lessons of modernity to understand Scripture better and the lessons of postmodernity to experience it deeply. We can, in faith, surrender to God, and then listen–to him and to each other–with patience and trust.

You will find no easy list of solutions in this book, no magic pill to make things better. The authors are certainly not asking you to imitate them. We fail as much as we succeed. But perhaps we can think together, talk together, and listen to one another. We will not give up our assumptions that there is absolute truth beneath it all. We are not willing to reject Scripture as God's fully-inspired word. We have no intention of compromising what we believe to be the heart of the Gospel, but we are convinced that we must look at how we think and how our cultural and intellectual environment has affected our thinking, and how that has influenced our understanding of Scripture and God. To do that, we have to examine our past to see how we got here. We have to unearth our assumptions and scrutinize them. And then, with humility, we can approach the holy writings of Scripture where we may find both our common ground and the central truths that transcend our culture and call us to surrender.

Chapter 3

The Christian at the Crossroads of Tradition and Culture

Remember the days of old;
Consider the generations long past.
Ask your father and he will tell you,
Your elders, and they will explain to you.
–Deuteronomy 32:7

Living in a House Built by Others

My family and I used to live in a house built in the sixteenth century. In that neighborhood, you couldn't help noticing that history touches the present. The house was a monument to the builders of long ago: three narrow stories located on a cobbled walk in the shadow of the remains of the old city wall. Inside, odd nooks that seemed to serve no purpose interrupted the plastered surfaces of the irregularly angled walls. The rooms had odd sizes and shapes. The ceilings were lumpy and the floors slanted crazily. How the builders of that era were able to make such stout castles and splendid manor homes, I'll never know. When they turned out to do a simple job like our little house, they somehow forgot how to use a plumb-bob and could no longer see straight. We were not surprised to learn that in the Middle Ages our neighborhood had been a slum, nicely situated in the fashionable sewer district just outside the city.

But at the end of the twentieth century it was a charming place in the center of Oxford, and we were the latest masters of this venerable home. Yet in some ways the house mastered us. Its historical peculiarities shaped our family life. Though the design and work of the original builders was centuries old, it left an impression on the present occupants' lifestyles. The steep and winding stairway we used every day was their idea, and because of it our toddlers routinely found themselves tumbling down to dinner rather than walking. Thanks to those builders our bathroom was one of the largest rooms in the house–large enough to have a climate of its own, a sort of permanent draft, very refreshing after a winter bath. We also enjoyed the galley kitchen they left us, so narrow and cramped that meal-time will forever seem a moment of rare intimacy in my family. But it was handy to be able to cook, wash, open the fridge (or the back door), and do the laundry, all from the kitchen table.

Our house was a standing tradition, a floor plan handed down to us from past generations, affecting our family life. It provided a solid framework that formed part of the structure of our lives. Yet it would be wrong to say that we were mere prisoners of the dizzy sixteenth-century designers, since their handiwork had been modified over the years and some functions had changed. After all, in their day the now-spacious bathroom would have been used for something else altogether. Indoor plumbing was introduced to the house fairly recently, as was a rotary telephone, electrical wiring, the ineffectual storage heaters and any number of other things–though in my wife's excellent judgment the carpeting appeared to have been original. We added a few small touches of our own–I wonder if the residents after us appreciated the remnants of crayon smudges on the bedroom wall?

The house is a product of the past, a tradition, a thing handed down. As such, it is partly static, a relic of the past, but it is also partly dynamic, changing to fit new circumstances and the needs of the latest occupants. During our time in the house, it was full of life. It nurtured life.

–Jeff

Why the Family House Frightens Us

Christians today often react to history and tradition in one of two ways: they either discard tradition because it's stifling and irrelevant, or they deny its value–perhaps even its existence–because they see it as human, as having no place in God's church. But as a people, we are the occupants of a house partly built by others. Part of the framework of our lives was hammered together by people long gone. We are shaped by the past, by people whose lives and experiences long ago touched some ancient stream of influence that slowly winds its way to us and subtly colors our present.

This is why we do history–to spot these streams and track them to our doorstep. As we investigate the past and think about the connections between events and persons, the outlines of the streams come into focus until we discover that we ourselves are in a moving flow of historical development. We have particular practices–and not others–because of circumstances in our past. We think in particular ways–and not in others–because of decisions made by people long ago.

These moments of realization can be unsettling. When we discover that history plays a big role in all our decisions, no matter how pure or innovative we believe ourselves to be, it can leave us feeling as if the past has a stranglehold on us. We feel like heirs to a house that can never be remodeled or changed. Or it scares us because it threatens to undercut the base of sacred assumptions. After all, history shows us that things start somewhere, sometime. This is fine for things like the steam engine or Communism, but it can be uncomfortable in our religion, when ideas or practices that we had assumed were totally "spiritual" and, like Melchizedek, apparently without origin, suddenly take a spot on the timeline. We're shocked to learn that they are part of history and tied to culture. This can be so alarming that we may opt to deny history, preferring to believe that everything about the house is divinely preordained and fixed, in every detail. No human carpenter needed.

Yet we are unavoidably the heirs to our past, no more able to escape from history than children are able to erase the evidence of their parents' influence. However we grow and change, we always carry with us a vestige of our origins, perhaps by being no more than a reaction in the opposite direction. Children who want to put some distance between themselves and their parents often show how much they owe to their parents' influence by their determined efforts to be different.

Life in the Orphanage: Possibilities and Problems

These observations shed some light on the mentality of the modern age. The children of the seventeenth and eighteenth centuries sought to distance themselves from their intellectual parents. Religious wars, narrow dogma, "unscientific" superstition, mindless oppression–this was the bitter legacy of the preceding generations. It seemed that the only way to escape the clutches of the past was to start over, from scratch. Philosophers tried to pare away the layers of prejudice handed to them out of the past, leaving only the individual's God-given intellect to seek truth. Scientists sought to liberate the world from ancient superstition by using a scientific method concerned only with the objective analysis of hard data. Artists and authors, weary of mimicking past masters, craved individual freedom of expression and the chance to create something totally new.

Since the past is unreliable, they reasoned–its methods suspect and its results flawed–who needs it? This is one reason why the ideals of individuality, independence, and originality have become like absolute values for us, norms to which we cling without even thinking. Our society lives by the slogan, "new is better," as if that were an obvious truth.

As it turns out, new is not always better; nor is *completely new* even possible. We cannot escape being shaped by our past. Though it may be useful at times to check our biases and traditions at the door in order to see things in a new way, we can never fully eliminate the influence of our past. In fact, the drive to do so has produced a kind of social neurosis in our world. Western society feels orphaned. By denying its past and its parents, it has deliberately orphaned itself, stifling the voice of its heritage by rubbing out *tradition* and acting as if it could somehow rise above history. As we saw in the last chapter, the impulse to start over is responsible for many of the great strides made in medicine and politics and technology. In a way, disconnecting from the past has paid off. Surely we are better off prescribing decent medicines rather than leeches. The gains have been considerable. But so have the costs. Living without a past has a price.

In our age, every generation feels the burden of reinventing itself. Since modern society convinces us that we have only two options–either mindlessly repeating past tradition or creating something novel–it's a no-brainer that we should go for "new and improved." Every generation struggles under the weight of this obligation to find its own truth and meaning, and in our society we have seen the symptoms of the despair it causes. A people without a history becomes a people lost and rootless. Our history is our memory; without memory we have no identity and are consigned to suffer a kind of self-imposed Alzheimer's. This is because, like it or not, we *are* part of a story larger than ourselves, and denial of this only creates disease.

In a cultural setting that puts such emphasis on starting fresh, it's not surprising that Churches of Christ have rushed into the orphanage. We have tended to minimize history and background in our practice of the Christian faith. The church, it seems, is no place for tradition.

Tradition is not a Four-Letter Word

Ironically, the inclination to live without a tradition has been one of the most prominent features of our tradition. This is partly because certain religious leaders of the early nineteenth-century movement out of which Churches of Christ emerged were heirs to an unhappy past. People like Alexander Campbell and Barton W. Stone looked around at the religious world and saw churches hopelessly bogged down in a swamp of stubborn traditions, encumbered by complex and often oppressive denominational doctrines and practices. They wanted to free churches from attitudes, doctrines, and practices they diagnosed as unhealthy. We're grateful for their liberating work and want to continue scrutinizing every practice and belief under the light of Scripture like they did. Yet doing so reveals that many traditions are good.

traditio (Latin)

the act of handing over or passing down; as when one generation gives its values and practices to the next generation

One of the reasons why many of our young people do not love our heritage more is that we have not taught them to love it. Symptomatic of this is our handling of the word *tradition*. In much of our preaching, the word has had only a negative meaning. So we lost an important word and trained ourselves to misunderstand it. Not all traditions are good, of course, but when we develop a knee-jerk reaction to the word itself instead of being thoughtful about it, we lose our grip on an important category of faith and make it all the harder to talk about something vital to the life of the church: the appreciation and appropriation of our history.

Our Tradition

In this context, by our tradition we mean the heritage of Churches of Christ–the set of attitudes, practices, forms, and doctrinal emphases historically characteristic of our movement in general.

Certainly Jesus and Paul were opposed to bad traditions, or even to the bad use of good ones (Matthew 15:1–9; Colossians 2:8). But the first-century church found that some traditions were crucial and worth handing down. Paul embraces certain traditions and uses them to good effect (1 Corinthians 11:2; 2 Thessalonians 2:15; 3:6), and it's worth noticing that when faced with a problem, he typically looks back to the formative Christian tradition for help, not towards novel programs and fresh approaches. In Scripture, the opposition is not between tradition and God's will, but between good tradition and bad tradition, bad tradition being that which undermines God's will.

Handling tradition is not a simple matter of labeling it flawed because it is human. We must also remember that God works among his people in history and leaves an imprint on our story, as he has ever done. Our traditions and history are partly the result of his activity among us and should not be treated dismissively. While tradition can be a harmful force because of human involvement, it can also be a positive force because of God's involvement. As we use the term *tradition* broadly in this book, we mean it neither as straightforward blessing or curse but recognize its potential to be either.

In view of our background, it's easy to see why we are so suspicious of tradition. *Traditionlessness*–the impulse to set out anew from wherever we stand as if it were a fresh starting point–has powerfully shaped our story. The early leaders of the Restoration Movement found that their ancestors had left them a house in which to live, but the floor plan was not to their liking and the construction seemed unreliable and dangerous. In keeping with the spirit of post-revolutionary America, their solution was to attempt to build a new house, to start over, building from the ground up.

A Religion of Historians

Unlike many thinkers of the day, the early leaders of the Movement, to their credit, chose not to begin with themselves as arbiters of truth. Instead, their starting point was the Bible. They placed great confidence in the ability of the human mind, but they placed even more in the Word of God in Scripture. Scripture would be the judge. If we stood on Scripture we could stand apart from the norms of human culture, they reasoned. In Scripture we could find the way to elevate true religion above the incidentals of the history that had gone so horribly wrong.

That they allowed Scripture to play such a role is praiseworthy. Their confidence in the ability of human reason to arrive at interpretations everyone would accept has turned out to be problematic, yet they demonstrated a humble and right attitude when they deliberately put themselves under Scripture and fearlessly began to examine everything by it. That is one of the best features of our heritage. They gave us a love for God's Word. They also recovered some biblical priorities, such as unity, the importance of baptism and the Lord's Supper–and the necessity of being wary of the dangers of arrogant self-righteousness.

Sadly, with that emphasis has often come a disregard for history. After all, the thinking goes, history and tradition are tainted with the physical, the human, the temporal, whereas the church must be founded on the spiritual, the transcendent, and the eternal. As for the span of centuries separating us from the time of the Apostles–skip it, downplay it. If it must come up, focus on its defects and errors. Be sure to point out that our goal is to be the pure church, with the messy problems of tradition and culture removed.

The problem is that, unlike in many other religions, *history is central to Christian belief.* Christianity emerges from historical events and constantly focuses on those points in time when God broke into the world to be redemptively involved in the lives of his people:

- Abraham's call
- the exodus
- the coming of Christ, etc.

Christianity cannot be boiled down to a state of mind or ethical principles. The truths of salvation are events, not just abstract ideas. History is essential and redemptive. For Christians, the historical events of Jesus' life, death, and resurrection form the core of Gospel truth and the foundation of authentic religion. To be Christian means letting the Lord make my story part of the larger story of God's past and present saving work in Christ. It means learning these events, connecting with their history, and re-appropriating them for life in baptism and discipleship. Christians spend their lives meditating on the events in the light of Scripture, reconnecting with them at times (e.g., when celebrating the Lord's Supper), and living out their significance. This is why it has been said that Christianity is a religion of historians.

It is also why Christianity will always take on some of the color and shape of its cultural context. Animal sacrifice, ritual meals, the kiss of greeting–all these practices existed in the surrounding culture before God's people adapted and used them under his guidance as we see in the Bible. Every style of music ever used in Christian worship has its roots in the musical norms of culture. Of course, connecting to culture can be dangerous for Christianity because the risk of accommodating, of selling out, is real. Nonetheless, the key to Christianity's redemptive power is in the church's ability to embody God's truth in the present world, as Jesus' ministry shows us. Christians have always believed that God's Word seeks to find fresh expression in every language, culture, and generation. The church cannot escape being partnered with human culture. "In the world but not of the world," we're called to be proclaimers of God's redemptive activity within our society.

Culture - Inescapable and Troubling

culture - "the sum total of ways of living built up by a group of human beings and transmitted from one generation to another"

–*Webster's Dictionary*

"Culture with us...ends in headache."

–*Ralph Waldo Emerson (1844)*

The formative thinkers of our movement believed this too, to an extent. But their greater emphasis was on the need to rise above history and culture in order to keep the church pure and abolish much of what had divided Christians and ruined churches. As it turns out, we did not achieve the splendid isolation from culture and history that we sought. Indeed, the very impulse to do so shows how deeply connected we have been to the streams and currents of our culture, because the desire to transcend history and to negate tradition is a product of the mood of those times.

Respecting our History as the Incarnation of God's Work

Recognizing that the church has a past, that it is necessarily influenced by human culture and tradition, does not mean that it is trapped as a merely human product. We should not devalue the faith and practice of our churches just because they've been shaped by historical circumstances. If Christian faith were about only the eternal and transcendent, how could it ever connect with us? We humans have something of the spiritual within us, but we are also time-bound and physical. We minister to real people in the real world and we can be glad that God meets us where we are. He chooses to work through human history and fallible people.

We are at this place and time partly because God has brought us here and some of the momentum we feel is the benevolent guidance of his hand reaching out to us through our ancestors in the faith. The goal is to recognize and appreciate God's work among us in the past, building on that momentum, while also 1) identifying points at which we have not been faithful and allowing God to reform us, and 2) adapting where appropriate to face the future faithfully but flexibly. It is crucial we understand that history is the incarnation of God's work.

> When as a child I heard the lofty language of the King James Version read aloud as God's Word, it seemed otherworldly to me, a direct speech from the Lord to my life and to our church.
>
> Years later I worked in the same Oxford College library that still houses the books Sir Henry Savile's team used when translating the book of Acts for the King James Version in the seventeenth century. The librarian, true to form, was thrilled to show me the collection. Now I know better how the King James originated and I have a more historically astute understanding of how the message of the Bible actually comes to us. No longer can I naively assume that the text appeared magically on the bookshelf, straight from God, because I have held in my hands some of the actual tools used by the flesh-and-blood people who translated it for me at a certain point in history. Does this mean those words are any less God's Word? Not at all; it means only that I understand a little better how God conveys his Word, that he does so by operating in history and through human beings.
>
> Recognizing the role of history and admitting that we are limited by our humanity does not bracket God out of the picture, as if he were unwilling to participate in anything human. The King James text of Acts is the Word of God; but it is also the translation of the sometime Warden of Merton College, Henry Savile.
>
> *–Jeff*

The finest expression of this is the incarnation of God's Word in the flesh (John 1:14), the exact representation of God in human form, Jesus Christ (Hebrews 1:3; Colossians 1:15; Philippians 2:6–7). Somehow in Jesus Christ divinity and humanity co-exist. Over the centuries many have argued about the mode and manner of this incarnation. Even if we do not understand fully how it all works, we affirm with Scripture that the one who got tired, wept, and bled (John 4:6; 11:35; 19:34) is also he who is one with the

Father, the eternal Word, and "God with us" (John 10:30; 1:1; Matthew 1:23). A mystery to be sure, but without it Christianity is pointless.

The church has some of the same mystery about it. The people in it are human and limited and make mistakes, yet the Lord works through them. Perhaps we have never explicitly denied that the church is both human and divine, but the ways we have typically handled history and tradition lead us to downplay the human dimension. It may not be easy to admit that circumstances and history should play any role in shaping the church, that the church is meant to be a combination of the divine and the human. Yet running scared from the notion actually undercuts what God is trying to do through the church–the place where the human encounters the divine for the sake of our redemption. The impulse to deny this "mixture" is akin to the impulse to deny either the divinity or humanity of Jesus. People who rejected the doctrine that the Son of God came in the flesh did so because they could not see how the divine and human can really co-exist (1 John 4:2–3). Of course, it is a mystery and a paradox. But the solution is not to collapse one side of the paradox for the sake of sitting comfortably with the other side, because it is somewhere between the two that God's work touches us.

In a sense, the church of our Lord is the second incarnation of Christ in the world (Romans 12:4–5; 1 Corinthians 12:12–27; Ephesians 1:23; 4:15–16, 25; 5:30; Colossians 1:24). But its human dimension consists not only of those who are presently walking the earth. The history of the church is the history of Christ's body as it moves through the centuries. Learning about our past is a way of studying our own anatomy and our family heritage, much of which

Learning Your Way around the Family Home

Some reasons to study your church's history:

- it is the incarnation of God's work
- it is the incarnation of Christ's body in action
- it is our background
- it is a teacher
- it is a source of stability and balanced perspective

has been shaped by God's creative hands. The church is a living, dynamic thing deeply enmeshed in history and culture as it carries out its redemptive mission. It is a body that moves through history. We are connected to its past as well as its present as we move toward the guarantee of future promise. We are the expression today of what God has been doing through his Son's body for some time. It makes sense that we take a reading on that momentum by knowing our history.

This puts the church's heritage into perspective. We have a story to guide us, in two parts. Our story is found not only in Scripture, but also in our history. This includes all the history of the church after the time of the Apostles and also the more recent history of our movement. In order to live out the church's story faithfully, we need to consult both accounts of the story, Scripture and heritage. They are not equal in authority: we rely on Scripture to judge our history as it has unfolded so far, validating parts of it, correcting other parts. We also seek to discern what new work God may be doing among us, since the Bible shows us that he is a God who delights in reviving and refreshing his people. Yet as we move forward to write the next portion of our story as God's people, we seek to do so in ways that are consistent with the full story.

A Voice out of the Past

Not all early leaders in the Restoration Movement had only harsh words for history and tradition. Though Alexander Campbell often railed against tradition because of the abuses he saw, he also appealed regularly to the larger Christian tradition in his arguments, finding some wisdom in the common mind of the church's history. He also warned that a campaign to eliminate everything human from the church would get out of hand.

In 1879, Burke Aaron Hinsdale, an Ohio preacher and college teacher in the Movement, published his *Ecclesiastical Tradition: Its Origin and Early Growth; Its Place in the Churches, and Its Value.* In it, Hinsdale surveyed the development and impact of tradition within the history of Christianity. He did not hesitate to blame many of the church's ills on the problems of tradition gone wrong, cautioning that tradition easily enslaves us and leads us away from God's will. However, he also pointed out that even churches of the Restoration Movement have a body of tradition. It is inevitable; our history and habits will always affect us–a fact dangerous to ignore.

Yet once we are aware of this, Hinsdale continued, we find there are benefits to be had by those who respect their history. We will be more stable because we maintain healthy continuity with the past. We can allow the positive momentum of past generations to carry through, while also being better trained to spot and block any negative currents that might threaten to sweep us off our course. Learning about our shortcomings is one of the benefits. Also, a look at history and tradition helps us discern the truly central doctrines of the faith, providing a big-picture view that will restrain us from putting too much stock in non-essentials. By both positive and negative examples, Hinsdale believed, tradition gives us perspective and challenges us to keep our priorities straight.

Respecting our History as Background and as Teacher

Hinsdale was right. We are inescapably bound to our story and a sense of heritage provides us with valuable resources for making wise decisions. For one thing, it helps to know our heritage because *history is background.* Over time people acquire traditional ways of thinking and doing things. When wheels run over the same course day after day they form ruts. Repetition becomes habit, habit becomes expectation. People may not respond well to changes in the routine–it destabilizes them, makes them feel uncomfortable. The way *we* do things can become *the* way to do things. Rituals adopted for the sake of convenience acquire almost divine status. To change or deviate from them is heresy.

> **Ritualism is no Substitute for Good Ritual**
>
> In her book, *Worship,* Evelyn Underhill says:
>
> "Ritualism represents the constant tendency of the human creature to attach absolute value to his own activities, whether personal or corporate: to assume that the precise way in which things are done is of supreme importance, and that the traditional formula has an inherent authority extending to its smallest details, from which it is blasphemy to depart."

Sensitive church leaders understand the principle of history-as-background and are cautious about changing set patterns, from the color of the bulletin to worship styles. They look for trends and habits, inquiring into the stories behind them. When they feel compelled to change something, they are patient and gentle so as to arouse the least amount of resistance and do the least damage possible. Like an intuitive counselor who inquires into the client's background and family history, they know that a healthy future may depend on knowing the past. For these reasons, effective ministry depends on learning a group's story–both the immediate history and the distant past. This approach to history has some pastoral wisdom, but it doesn't go far enough. A church's history is not just a kind of inertia that we must overcome in order to make progress.

A second practical approach to our history views it more positively, respecting *history as teacher*. Given a voice, the past will teach us valuable lessons. It will challenge us to evaluate our priorities, help us put things into perspective, give us balance, and teach us something about what works and what does not–and how to respond maturely in either case. Far from stifling creativity, history has the potential to suggest creative alternatives we would never have dreamed up on our own. However, the past acquires its best voice only when we seek out and listen to the stories of yesterday's people. If we listen closely we will learn so much more than useful points of view on doctrine, practice, and ministry; we will hear the voices of hearts seeking God's presence, the sounds of prayer, the melody of praise, the quiet movement of hands in service. We will find companions and long-lost family members and be glad to share with them our common spiritual journey.

Not that the past was always right or that everything done in the past is to be imitated now. As always, Scripture must guide our priorities. Nevertheless, our ministry for the Kingdom is richer when the lessons we've received from our heritage form the backdrop against which we serve. Otherwise, we're cutting ourselves off from one of our God-given resources for wisdom. Especially in times of great change or difficulty, great discernment is needed. Ignoring the tutor of history is irresponsible.

Disrespect as a Hobby

All this means we need to respect our history by finding ways in our churches to explore it as the work of God. This is easy to say but harder to follow. We have developed a hobby of historical neglect. For some, truly coming to grips with the fact that we have a history has shattered confidence in our heritage. This need not happen. Perhaps we have not paid enough attention to how God really works, nor equipped ourselves to respect our humanity and our history for what it is and be grateful to God for it.

Christians in Churches of Christ are standing at the crossroads of tradition and culture, facing a tough choice: to respect our history or not. If we choose not to respect our history, we greatly impoverish our churches and the Lord's work. Yet the temptation to disrespect history is as great for "traditionalists" as it is for "progressives." Each perspective has its own angle, but the two typical ways of disrespecting history have surprisingly similar outlooks on tradition.

Tradition vs. Traditionalism

Tradition is the living faith of the dead. Traditionalism is the dead faith of the living. And, I suppose I should add, it is traditionalism that gives tradition such a bad name.

–Jaroslav Pelikan

One way to disrespect history drinks deep of the modern anti-historical mindset we discussed above, either denying that earthly history has had any effect on the Lord's true church or insisting that whatever effect it has had is illegitimate and ought to be overcome and erased. There is a sinister danger here. Far from eliminating tradition, this attitude forces tradition underground, where it operates freely, unidentified and unchecked. What was vital tradition becomes oppressive *traditionalism*. Traditions that grew out of specific circumstances are presumed to be absolute and eternal in their significance, making it difficult to distinguish practices at the core of God's will for a Christ-centered church from those that lie at the periphery. Such an attitude inevitably leads to sectarian divisions, as we exalt our patterns as fully divine, displaying an arrogant rejection of any who differ.

Disrespecting our history in this way causes us to cling tightly to our traditions without recognizing them as such. We become traditionalists. And especially in times of great cultural change we are left without the tools to cope, retreating instead into a memory of the "good old days," rendering the heritage stale and wooden. We may be reduced to lonely despair or incited to fiery proclamation against the growing apostasy. Yet since we deny the existence of something so real–our own time-bound story and culture–we set ourselves up for a fall.

The fall may come at the hands of those who choose another way to disrespect history, a way that actually comes out of the same ideals, but moves in a different direction. This happens when we admit that tradition exists in the church but still buy into the idea that it is strictly human. We know we have a history, but we devalue and dismiss it. Anything traditional is inconsequential unless it is immediately practical. Since tradition is time-bound, it is relatively unimportant and can be changed on a whim.

When we adopt this perspective, we actually become much like our forefathers, seeking to be freed from the limits of history by denying the powerful and redemptive role it plays. In fact, the bias can become so strong that merely doing things in non-traditional ways can seem like breathing fresh air and a "progressive" agenda can seem like the best expression of the Gospel's freedom. We are likely to pursue programs that take little or no account of our heritage, without investing the time to discover what divine wisdom may have shaped that heritage or what lessons it may have to teach us. When we disrespect history in this "ultra-progressive" way, we're liable to see no value in letting our history illuminate the specific paths by which God has called us to fulfill our mission. Rather than respectfully and attentively listening to our parents' voices, we are happy to live as orphans.

Ironically, the very heritage we're trying to abandon often sets the agenda. Like adolescent children, we are liable to act out against our parents when we feel their restrictive oversight lying too heavily upon us. We do the opposite of what they tell us. Yet we become more enslaved to the tradition than we realize as we seek to satisfy the craving to do everything differently. The tradition still calls the shots, only in a reverse way. In spite of all the effort to ditch the shackles of tradition and run free, the tradition lives on, lurking beneath the surface as a thing to be reacted against, exerting unbridled influence on the church amidst a climate of denial. Because we do not bother to know *who we were* we do not know *who we are.* No healthy identity exists.

Perhaps worst of all, we come to understand *church* to mean the *church present.* The *church past* doesn't count, nor does *church future* count for much. We forget that the stories of today will soon become the stories of yesterday. We are making history. If we continue our habit of losing touch with yesterday, we're leaving our children no inheritance. When we abandon the structures of nurture that keep the faith communities of past, present, and future dynamically linked up, the obsession with *now* forces *yesterday* and *tomorrow* to the margins. Or off the page.

This anti-tradition reaction to a "traditionless" tradition does not leave us standing on solid ground. Instead, what we applaud as pure spiritual revival may turn out to be a combination of situation-specific attitudes and practices driven largely by one generation's reaction to a disowned past. Such a reaction may be well-meaning and fresh, but it cannot be as solidly grounded on deep spiritual foundations as it might be if it hadn't muted its parents' voices. Even if we could achieve the goal of complete liberation from history, the reward would be only a crippling disorientation, with the result that the ship's rudder may be handed over to whichever governing force will grab it first and firmest–contemporary marketing strategies, the idol of measurable church growth effectiveness, sheer reactiveness, the personal agendas of charismatic leaders–all are ready candidates. Since we cannot actually live as orphans, we adopt illegitimate parents.

Two Effective Ways to Disrespect Tradition:

1) Pretend it does not exist
2) Pretend it should not exist

Both the "traditionalist" and "ultra-progressive" responses disrespect history, one cleaving to its heritage in a way that invites the other to abandon its heritage. Both understand history as basically negative, not as the ongoing sequel to the story of Scripture. Neither side offers much hope of fostering maturity in the church. Neither one provides a means of linking family generations together in a healthy way. By not respecting the power and force of history as a part of the fabric of God's work, both responses intentionally close their eyes to the positive gains of heritage while camouflaging its dangers so that they operate freely under the surface, unacknowledged and out of control.

The irony is that the "traditionalist" response is not very different from the "ultra-progressive" one in its understanding of our heritage. At first glance, they look very different–the one forcefully (and unconsciously) maintaining its heritage as it cries out loudly against the other's high-throttle abandonment of that heritage–but the responses of both are actually propelled by an incomplete view of heritage.

Conclusion: Time for History

The reader may have been wondering why a book about church identity and direction did not begin at the beginning: with the Bible and God's lasting plan for the Christian and the Church. Why not lay out the timeless principles of God's truths first, then apply them?

We hope that by this point the reason is becoming clear: as humans we have no choice but to begin where we are. No one can begin at the beginning. God is timeless and he is Truth, but we are neither. When we come to the Bible, we come from where we stand. Although God's Word lays a claim on us to transform us, it is a claim that we appropriate from where we are in history and culture. We have wanted this book to proceed in a way that recognizes this.

Other readers may wonder why we did not begin with the important matters–church mission and renewal at the grassroots level, practical ministry. After all, the up-and-coming generation is not particularly concerned with history. Given the present decline of "denominational loyalties" and general suspicion of traditional institutions, rehearsing history is a waste of time, some might say. Let's spend our energies on things that will reach people and grow churches.

We understand this concern for practical ministry; it is a passion we share also, but our response is two-fold. First, beware of over-generalizing. Things are not so plain. Although it's true that many people are not excited spiritually by history and tradition, the fact that certain extremely traditional institutions–like the Orthodox Church in America–are experiencing dramatic growth right now should warn us against painting our picture with broad brush strokes. No one profile actually fits the whole "up-and-coming generation." Many people in our increasingly rootless society are looking for roots.

Second, as we have tried to show in this chapter, tradition and history are as real as the air we breathe, whether we are aware of it or not. When seekers are drawn to the shape and style of a particular church, however contemporary its focus, they are drawn to something that is the product of that church's past and its traditions. One way or another, a church's history is a part of its life, its appeal, its service. Even if non-Christians have no pressing desire to be aware of history, church leaders cannot be so shortsighted. Concerned with the business of discernment and with helping the family of faith mature, leaders often find the advice of the grandparents to be more helpful than that of the children–especially when the grandparents are willing to speak their time-proven counsel in language the grandchildren can appreciate. God's continued activity in our midst moves us to tell the ongoing story of what he has done since the time of Jesus, just as we hope to pass on to the next generation some sense of how God has worked among us in our own time.

Nevertheless, we must admit that the goal of knowing heritage is not immediately practical. Knowing our story is a matter of spiritual formation. The gains of knowing heritage come in the form of shaping attitudes and imparting wisdom, of building character and promoting maturity, of enriching our language of praise as we identify God's past work among us, of cultivating a means of nurturing the next generation. Impractical? Perhaps–by contemporary American standards, at least. The processes of spiritual formation do not produce instantly measurable results. Yet the cultivation of our souls must be the foundation of everything we do. Like the Jews of Jesus' time, who by observing Passover connected themselves to their past and enriched their present, our faith will be more solid and productive as we respectfully celebrate our own heritage.

Even if the aims of respecting our history are not immediately practical, there are some practical means of cultivating that respect. Church leaders will do well to find creative and engaging ways to explore, rehearse, and appropriate the stories of their churches. They can design classes that teach the story of God's people since Bible times, including the stories of the Restoration Movement and the more local history of their own congregation. They can ensure that every child in the church is able to recount briefly how the story of their church connects to the larger story of God's people. Churches should put a priority on intergenerational activities. Public gatherings provide opportunities for people to tell their stories, the stories of God's activity, giving us a chance to join the amazing personal stories of the present with those of the past. We may find that our exploration of history supplies us with so many compelling resources that we cannot help but interweave the images, language, and heroic tales of the past with our preaching and teaching, our mission statements, and the artwork in our publications.

As a people, we are pursuing the plot line of a story that includes human and divine elements, as it should. Our family home is a good one; we can be excited about the future. Before we as a heritage move on to the next phase of our story, it would be useful to review how our story has developed so far and consider how that past narrative will inevitably make a major impression on the drama as it unfolds further. By doing so, we may be able to step into the future with a more mature and faithful stance than would be possible if we either blindly abandon our heritage or blindly behave as if history and tradition does not exist among us.

Chapter 4

Family Resemblances: Why Do We Have Blue Eyes?

How shall we labor with any effect to build up the church, if we have no thorough knowledge of her history, or fail to apprehend it from the proper point of observation? History is, and must ever continue to be, next to God's Word, the richest fountain of wisdom, and the surest guide to all successful practical activity.

–Phillip Schaff

At first glance I thought it was one of those fake old-time photos you can get at any amusement park. You know, where you and your family dress up in old outfits and pay for a sepia-toned family photo. When I picked it up from the box, though, I could tell it was not a fake. It was a very old picture of my mother. The smile, the eyes, the way she held her shoulders all confirmed it was her.

But something was a little confusing. The surrounding scenery in the picture–the house, the lawn, the horse-drawn buggy, the clothes–were all from an era much earlier than my mother's time. I was mistaken. There was no way it could really be her. But it *was* her!

My aunt entered the room and saw my puzzled look. Realizing what I had in my hand she explained with a laugh, "That's a picture of your great grandmother. She died before you were born, but your mother is as like her as anyone could be." I stared at the photo for a long time. The features my mother had inherited from her grandmother were striking. Even more striking to me right then was the realization that before that moment I had known nothing at all about how profoundly my great grandmother had contributed to my mother's looks and mannerisms.

My mother was not simply a duplicate of her ancestor. She had formed a unique personality out of a lifetime of her own experiences and choices. But there was no mistaking it–my mother had received much of who she was from that relative of generations past.

It never crossed my mind to think less of my mother now that I knew how significantly she had been shaped by this ancestor. Such a reaction would have been absurd. Instead, I wanted to know more about this relative, and all my ancestors, so I could understand better where we had come from. I wasn't just interested in facial features and body shapes, I wanted to know about our family customs and internal dynamics so I could see those family resemblances too. The experience opened my eyes to the reality of past shaping the present.

–Doug

If you traced the spiritual ancestry of Churches of Christ, you would be right to start with the people of the Bible, the followers of God in the Old Testament and the New. If we can't connect ourselves intimately with them, something is certainly wrong. However, when we look for family resemblances in more recent relatives, we begin to recognize definite features in the 1500s, the era of the Protestant Reformation. The similarities are sometimes striking, like looking at cousins at a family reunion where facial features, hair color, and body shape make it clear they belong in the family too! The same is true of our spiritual ancestors who lived during and after the Reformation, the similarities between us and them are undeniable.

This chapter does not take an exhaustive look at every trait we have inherited. Nor do we mean to imply that we are helpless products of what we received from our ancestors. Instead, we have tried to create a sense of why we are the way we are–of why we have blue eyes instead of brown, so to speak–so we can appreciate the strengths we have inherited in this spiritual lineage and deal with the weaknesses in a healthy and godly way. Our spiritual and intellectual ancestors are a fascinating and complex bunch that includes Calvinists and Arminians, Puritans and Anabaptists, European intellectuals, and American popularizers. Tracing out every line of descent is not always easy, but it is an exciting and rewarding task–as anyone who has ever become captivated by their genealogy can attest. Let's take a look at what some of those fascinating relatives looked like.

Churches of Christ belong to the lineage of the Protestant Reformation. Those great-grandparents in the faith caught a vision of what the church should be in contrast to the way they saw it in their day. While none believed the church could ever cease to exist, it had been terribly corrupted by unworthy leaders who placed their own selfish interests ahead of Christ. Church offices that provided huge salaries and political power, too often had become prizes for sale to the highest

Inherited Reformation Traits

The Protestant Reformation is one of the most splendid eras in the history of the world, and will long be regarded by the philosopher and the philanthropist as one of the most gracious interpositions in behalf of the whole human race. We Americans owe our national privileges and our civil liberties to the Protestant reformers. They achieved not only an imperishable fame for themselves, but a rich legacy for their posterity... we are indebted to the intelligence, faith, and courage of Martin Luther and his heroic associates in that glorious reformation.

–Alexander Campbell,
Preface to *The Christian System*

bidder. Pardon for sin, it seemed, could be purchased too; and the so-called religious people who took vows of poverty and sexual purity often appeared to be richer and less pure than anyone.

The reformers wanted to reclaim Christ's church from those who were abusing it, to bring it into submission to God's will so that he could cleanse its blemishes and give it back the glory it was meant to have. The German monk Martin Luther (1483-1546) gets credit for beginning the Reformation. In October 1517 he nailed a set of ninety-five theses or propositions for debate to the door of the University church where he preached in Wittenberg, Germany. These propositions attacked the doctrine of indulgences which were pardons for sin issued by the church in exchange for acts of repentance–often a donation of money. Luther went on to examine Roman Catholic teaching on issues ranging from authority in the church to singing in worship. Eventually he stated the Reformation principles of "Scripture alone," "grace alone," "faith alone," and the priesthood of all believers. The movement he began would eventually spread across most of northern Europe and spawn other reform movements across the continent and the world.

The Reformed Branch of the Family

But it was another reformer with a different approach to the church's problems who would contribute more to the "gene pool" of Churches of Christ than Luther. Ulrich Zwingli (1484-1531) began the "Reformed" part of the Protestant Reformation with his work in Zurich, Switzerland. By the time Zwingli was ordained a priest in 1506 he was already an admirer of the Catholic reformer Desiderius Erasmus who was attacking abuses in the church through his writings. When Zwingli was chosen preacher for the main church in

Zurich in December 1518, he began a career that would lead to a break with Catholicism and a reformulation of key Christian doctrines.

Zwingli was convinced through his reading of Erasmus that the real source of authority for Christian doctrine was Scripture, not the commentaries and lectionaries produced by the Catholic Church. So in January 1519, he announced that he would simply begin preaching through the New Testament. It wasn't long before his sermons were filled with attacks on monasticism, Purgatory, and praying to saints. When he wrote a tract saying that Christians should be freed from the control of the Pope and bishops, the Catholic archbishop over Zurich moved to stop Zwingli's work. Instead, Zwingli successfully defended sixty-seven articles before the City Council, leading to Zurich's break from Roman Catholicism.

Two of Zwingli's views are particularly important to us in Churches of Christ because they are part of our inheritance: his understanding of the silence of Scripture, and his doctrine of the Lord's Supper. Zwingli, unlike Luther, believed that if the Bible did not specifically authorize a practice, the church must reject it. This strict view led him to renounce, among other things, instrumental music in worship. He even prohibited singing in worship since he could find no command for it in Scripture. Zwingli had a hard time following this principle when some of his own church members pointed out that infant baptism was not mentioned in Scripture either. Yet this "restrictive" approach to the silence of Scripture became an important legacy to his descendants in the Reformed tradition, including Churches of Christ.

For Zwingli, the focus of the Lord's Supper was on the Spirit of Christ and what Christ had done for humanity, not on the physical elements of the bread and wine. While all the reformers rejected the Roman Catholic idea that the elements changed into the literal body and blood of Christ, Lutherans still believed in a special presence of Christ's body in the bread and wine. Zwingli was convinced that attributing any special qualities to the physical elements could become idolatry.

He insisted, instead, that worship is entirely spiritual–we don't need to rely on physical objects to worship God. Zwingli's view is often called "memorialism," the idea that the Lord's Supper is simply an occasion to think about what Christ has done for us. Zwingli's teaching was actually more complex than that. He believed the Lord's Supper was a deeply spiritual act. But he could not accept the idea that Christians receive the Spirit of Christ by eating this physical food. The bread and wine were symbols that represented the body and blood, which reminded Christians of God's act of salvation for us. In his attacks on other understandings of the Lord's Supper he often does seem to be "a bare memorialist." Once again, this trait was passed on to several groups with ancestry in the Reformed tradition, including Churches of Christ.

> Our Father in heaven, we thank you for this bread which represents to us the broken body of our Lord and Savior on the cruel cross of Calvary. May we partake of it in a manner that is well pleasing to you.
>
> In like manner, we give thanks for this fruit of the vine, which represent to us the shed blood of our Lord and Savior Jesus Christ on the cross. May we partake of it in a worthy manner.
>
> *–Lord's Supper prayer in Churches of Christ*

Zwingli's contributions to the Reformation were extremely important. But it was John Calvin (1509-1564) in Geneva who would become the main source of Reformed teaching and practice. Calvin's influence on this part of the Reformation was so strong that "Calvinist" practically became a synonym for "Reformed." His thought is still influential, though Calvin would likely not be happy with everything that came to be called Calvinism. Yet the bottom line for Calvin and the key element in all Reformed theology is a belief in the absolute sovereignty of God. God is ultimately, completely and solely in charge of everything.

Calvin and the other reformers believed that the medieval church had given people the impression they could manipulate God. One could take care of sins by performing acts of "penance" like reciting prayers, burning candles, making pilgrimages, or donating money to the church. Sometimes it seemed that the penance prescribed was designed more to enrich powerful church leaders than to bring sinners to spiritual health. When Calvin emphasized God's sovereignty, he was making the point that humans do not control God. God will do what God chooses to do regardless of what humans do or do not do. The doctrine of predestination became a key part of the "Reformed" package, teaching that although all humans deserve damnation, God has chosen to save some based on nothing more than His sheer grace and mercy. Nothing we say or do has any affect whatsoever on God's sovereign choice.

It may seem strange, but Calvin meant this doctrine as a comfort to Christians. No one can snatch us out of God's hand. Our salvation is secure even if we mess up, because it depends on God's work, not ours. The other side of the coin, however, was, in Calvin's own words, "a terrible decree." If you were not among the ones God selected for salvation, there was no remedy.

It was not until half a century after Calvin's death that

"Calvinism" took the form most people know today. In the early 1600s James Arminius (1560-1609), a professor at the Reformed theological school at Leiden in the Netherlands, challenged several major Calvinist teachings. He rejected the ideas that humans were unable to turn to God and that Christ died only for the elect. Arminius and his followers insisted that God had given every person enough grace, enough ability, to turn to God if they chose to. "Arminianism" still put a heavy emphasis on the sovereignty of God and the basic helplessness of human beings. In that sense it was still part of "Reformed" theology. Yet it rejected the harsh Calvinist notion that human beings had absolutely no part in determining their own eternal destiny.

After Arminius's death, his followers drew up a list of five points of disagreement with the Calvinists. However, at a council held at Dort in 1618 and 1619, the Calvinists passed five articles that directly contradicted each of the Arminian points. This list from the Synod of Dort became the famous five points of Calvinism that in English is often put into the acronym TULIP.

Total Depravity – humans are completely depraved, having no ability to respond to God; they can do nothing good.

Unconditional Election – God has elected or selected certain people to be saved without any conditions whatsoever.

Limited Atonement – Christ died only for the elect.

Irresistible Grace – if you are among the elect, you cannot resist God's grace–he will save you.

Perseverance of the Saints – also known as "once saved, always saved." God's elect will endure.

Inherited Calvinist and Arminian "genes" would again become the source of fierce conflict in America. Most Protestants who came to the new world were from European churches that were thoroughly Calvinist. But many American pioneers who had wrested a life for themselves from the hostile wilderness simply could not accept the idea that they had no say at all in where they would spend eternity. Among the doctrine's strongest opponents were the ministers who became the founding leaders of the Stone-Campbell Movement.

As Barton Stone reflected on his life's work in his autobiography, he lashed out at Calvinism as "among the heaviest clogs on Christianity in the world. It is a dark mountain between heaven and earth, and is amongst the most discouraging hindrances to sinners from seeking the Kingdom of God, and engenders bondage and gloominess to the saints." Alexander Campbell made fun of the Calvinist idea that God would suddenly convert people out of the blue regardless of where and who they were.

At first it seems like the Reformed gene we inherited was just not compatible with American blood–our early leaders appeared to reject Calvinism completely. But things are not that simple. True, the nineteenth-century leaders of Churches of Christ rejected any idea of a God who arbitrarily chose some to be saved and others to be lost. Yet they

> These elect infants, elect pagans, elect idiots, on whom God acts when, where, and how he pleases, but makes them holy in a moment, without light, knowledge, faith, or love, are figments of distempered brains, the creatures of religious romance, the rare offspring of a metaphysical delusion, for which there is no cure but in the rational reading and study of the book of God.
>
> *–Campbell-Rice Debate, 1843*

still held to God's sovereignty, and some even to the inability of humans to do good on their own. So exactly how do we trace our ancestry to the Reformed tradition? What is the genealogical link between Reformed thought and the Stone-Campbell Movement?

Our Puritan Cousins

The most direct relatives of Churches of Christ from the Reformed tradition are undoubtedly the Puritans. Puritan ideas emerged in several places not long after the first wave of the Reformation, but it was in England that Puritanism got its name and organization. Basically they believed that the English Reformation had not gone far enough. To these Puritans, even the Church of England still needed to be purified from corruptions its leaders had allowed to continue. Most worked from the inside to bring about the changes they believed were needed.

One group of English Puritans is an especially significant set of ancestors for Churches of Christ. This body focused on the English church's organization and government as one of its most pressing problems. The Church of England still had the medieval structure in which powerful bishops ruled the church. This group of Puritans insisted that the church leaders depicted in Scripture were not bishops empowered from on high to rule the church, but congregational elders ("presbyters" in Greek). Calvin and others who set up groups of elders as decision-making bodies in every church and region had influenced these Presbyterians. The Presbyterians never succeeded in getting their ideas permanently in place in the Church of England. But their ideas won the day in the Scottish Reformation. When the Church of Scotland was organized in 1560 it was organized as a Presbyterian church–a church ruled by elders.

All the major thought shapers of the early Stone-Campbell Movement were Presbyterians. Thomas Campbell and Barton W. Stone were ordained Presbyterian ministers, Campbell in a branch of the Church of Scotland, Stone in the Presbyterian Church in the United States of America. Alexander Campbell was thoroughly tutored in the Presbyterian faith by his father. They all knew the Reformed theology of Presbyterianism, especially its chief English-language creed, the Westminster Confession of Faith (1646). And they all believed that elders in each congregation were the leaders authorized by Scripture.

Though the Presbyterians rejected the idea of bishops with power over the whole church, they did maintain a strong sense of connection between congregations. They established regional and national assemblies of elders to ordain ministers and settle conflicts. Some other Puritans, however, went much further in their rejection of medieval church organization. They insisted that each congregation was entirely independent of every other congregation. For many years a minister named Robert Browne (1550-1633) was a vocal spokesperson for this brand of "separatism." He was so convinced that the Church of England could not be reformed that he began organizing congregations free from any connection to the government. The English authorities regarded such actions as dangerous to the stability of society. It was almost impossible for people then to conceive of a situation where the church and state were not intimate partners.

After being imprisoned several times, Browne and his followers moved to the Netherlands. In 1582 he wrote a famous tract titled "A Treatise of Reformation Without Tarrying for Any," explaining his views of biblical church government. The church consists of local congregations of believers voluntarily united to Christ and to each other. Furthermore, each congregation is to choose its own ministers and officers without any external interference. Though many separatists were jailed, exiled, or executed, their ideas of congregational autonomy would eventually become the norm in many American churches.

Of even more direct ancestry is the work and thought of the Scottish Independent John Glas (1695-1771). Glas, a minister of the Church of Scotland, came to the conclusion that no civil magistrate or government could exercise power over the church if Christ is truly its king. Glas was devoted to Scripture as the only rule for all Christian beliefs and practices. He insisted on, among other things, a plurality of elders in each local congregation, and weekly observance of the Lord's Supper. These ideas and others promoted by Scottish Independents influenced both Thomas and Alexander Campbell in the years before they came to America.

Oversight by elders in independent local congregations is an important part of the identity of Churches of Christ. And there is no question that these practices were passed down to us through our Presbyterian and Independent Puritan ancestors. But the Presbyterians did not invent rule by elders, nor did the separatists create congregational church organization. Those "genes" did not originate with them. The early church practiced these things in some fashion. But it is a serious mistake to miss the fact that our emphasis on these matters and the particular way we have handled them have been shaped by our connections to people living long after the time of the early church. To assume that everything we believe and practice came straight from the text of Scripture is to ignore the human channels through which they came to us and through which God works.

Recognizing Our Ancestry

As Alexander Campbell worked through doctrinal issues in his new reformation, he almost always included an in-depth discussion of what past believers had to say. He always made it clear that he believed Scripture was the final authority for any doctrine. And sometimes when he quoted past religious leaders it was to give examples of teachings he rejected. The point is that it mattered to Campbell what Christians through the centuries had thought. He knew that the legacy of those past generations had formed the beliefs of his own age. He studied those ideas–not so he could blindly duplicate them–but to discover and reexamine the traits he had inherited and to take advantage of the accumulated wisdom of those spiritual ancestors who had struggled to follow Christ through the ages. Though Campbell sometimes had a hard time admitting he had been influenced by the ideas of others, especially when those others were regarded as "heretics," even his hedging indicates his debt.

> While I thus acknowledge myself a debtor to [Robert and James Haldane and Robert Sandeman-Scottish Independents], I must say that the debt, in most instances is a very small one. I am indebted, upon the whole, as much to their errors as to their virtues,...the largest amount of my debt is of this kind, though in some instances I have been edified and instructed in their labors.
>
> I have endeavored to read the Scriptures as though no one had read them before me; and I am as much on my guard against reading them today, through the medium of my own views yesterday, or a week ago, as I am of being influenced by any foreign name, authority or system, whatever.
>
> –Alexander Campbell, *Christian Baptist*, 1826

The things that Campbell and other leaders of the Movement came to believe concerning church organization and the Lord's Supper are not surprising–they reflect the theology of their Reformed ancestors. Admitting this does not diminish the validity of any of those positions. It merely acknowledges the obvious–that we are human and cannot help being influenced by those who have come before us. Despite Campbell's statement above, human beings simply cannot detach themselves from all prior human thought and create their beliefs and practices as if nothing had been done before. Many of our most basic beliefs–our emphasis on Scripture, our rejection of predestination, our emphasis on congregational rule by elders and congregational autonomy–all have precedents in the Reformed thought of the sixteenth and seventeenth centuries.

The early leaders of the Restoration Movement knew their spiritual genealogy. They also knew the Scriptures and believed that the *ultimate* source of their beliefs and practices had to be God himself speaking through the Scriptures. Our Reformed relatives were channels of many of our ideas and practices. We thank God for the blessing of this ancestry, but we recognize that they were the "clay vessels" of God's work, imperfect instruments in his hands–just as we are. To ignore this may cause us to miss the ways that God is moving among us now to reform and perfect us.

The Anabaptist Branch of the Family

Another important group of ancestors of Churches of Christ are the Anabaptists. Like the Puritans, the Anabaptists were born of Reformed parents. This branch of the family, however, developed a theology very different from Calvinist beliefs.

Some members of Ulrich Zwingli's congregation in Zurich had

taken him seriously when he told them to study the Scriptures for themselves and refuse to let the church dictate how they understood them. When a group began to question infant baptism and church-state connections, Zwingli balked. After all, it was the Zurich city council that had given him the political support he needed to carry out his reforms. After these Anabaptists (re-baptizers) lost a debate with Zwingli before the council, they were ordered to have their children baptized immediately or face severe penalties. Many moved out of Zurich to start their own "free" church in a town to the south named Zollicon. Government officials pursued them and within a few years had executed many of their leaders, often by drowning.

The Anabaptists made radical adjustments to the way they understood the church. Lutheran and Reformed theology saw the church in light of Jesus' parable of the wheat and the weeds (Matthew 13:25-40). The weeds were left in the field with the wheat until the harvest because pulling them any earlier would destroy much of the wheat too. Since the other Reformation churches practiced infant baptism like the Roman Catholics, everyone was "in the church." That meant, however, that many church members were Christians in name only. These reformers admitted the visible church might include many who would not be saved. But the separation of the wheat from the weeds, the saved from the unsaved, was not the job of the church but of God at the final judgment.

But to the Anabaptists the church was not a field with wheat and weeds, but the pure bride of Christ described in Ephesians 5. Some of them described it as a bolt of white cloth that would be ruined if one flawed thread were introduced. They rejected the Lutheran and Reformed teaching of the total depravity and inability of humans.

Instead, they insisted that people could accept Christ as savior and live a life of holiness and service. Furthermore, only those who had accepted Christ and been converted were eligible for baptism–not infants. The Christian must then live a life of strict holiness or suffer the ban–excommunication for the purpose of rehabilitation. Even more than the Arminians of the next century, the Anabaptists focused on what people could and ought to do rather than on what they couldn't.

These peaceful "Swiss Brethren" held up the ideal of living lives of holiness and worship in churches free from control by governments and church hierarchies. Their practice of adult baptism, eventually by immersion, became a powerful witness to the practice of the early church in their day. These relatives are "once removed" from our direct line of descent. The genes we inherited of respect for authority of Scripture, practice of believer's baptism, and emphasis on individual holiness came most directly through other lines. Yet there is no question that we bear a strong family resemblance to the Anabaptists in profound ways.

Our Inheritance of Concern for Christian Unity

Though it had never been the reformers' intention to divide the church, as the Reformation progressed it became terribly apparent that the church had fragmented. Most frightening to some reformers was the realization that they were at least partly responsible for the division, a direct violation of the Lord's last prayer for his followers. For a few, especially among the radicals and separatists, there was no problem. For them the church had ceased to exist in the visible Catholic Church–it was not the church at all. There had been no division in the church, just a separation of true Christians from false ones. Still, most reformers struggled with the problem of unity. How could the church be cleansed from the corruptions it suffered and still be visibly united?

The Lutheran leader Philip Melanchthon (1497-1560) was willing to compromise with Roman Catholics on what he called "non-essential" matters–matters neither commanded nor condemned in Scripture–to keep the German churches united. Some "true Lutherans" opposed Melanchthon, insisting that no compromise was possible. Although the "true Lutherans" agreed that some things in Christianity were more important than others, they insisted that once you had all the parts of true teaching and practice in place, you had to defend everything as a package. Everything stood or fell together. Those who disagreed with any part of the package were lost.

This trait has shown up frequently in Churches of Christ, but our Lutheran relatives are not the only ones who carried that gene. Our first cousins the Puritans, though their greatest concern was the purity of the church, also struggled with the tension between being right and being united. Much like the "true Lutherans," separatist Puritans saw themselves as the only true Christians. Any who claimed to be followers of Christ in the "apostate churches" were not Christians at all.

But not all Puritans were so exclusive. Though they wouldn't go as far as Melanchthon in permitting a wide range of "non-essentials," some Puritans believed that a practice not mentioned in the Bible might be permissible if it was in accord with the general aims of Scripture to glorify God and edify His people. Not all congregations had to do it, but congregations that did could not be considered apostate. These Puritans were still very reluctant to add to or modify their beliefs and practices, but they allowed for more leeway than their more rigid sisters and brothers. This trait too is part of our inheritance from the Puritans, though it has often been overpowered by the more rigid exclusivist gene.

One way people tried to solve the problem of the divisions caused by the Reformation was to talk about the "invisible church." No one believed that the church had ceased to exist, even when the visible body looked its worst. Christ had promised that his church would never fall–that the gates of hell itself would not prevail against it (Matthew 16:18). Even the separatists had to admit that. But now the church was horribly divided. A mix of religious and political issues was leading to wars and persecutions more vicious than ever before. Yet if the *invisible* church *was* united–united in the mind of God–then what appeared to be a great division was really no division at all.

This idea was certainly not new. It's one of the ways Scripture portrays the church. The statement in Acts 2:47 that the Lord added to the church those who were being saved implies that ultimately God alone knows who is in and who is out. The reformers believed there are visible marks that identify a true church pleasing to God and which humans cannot ignore. But the true church–the church that God alone knows–may include many who are not in a church with these marks and may exclude many who are. The key was that the invisible church *was* united in the mind of God where it really counted. For some, this was the solution to the division problem. You must do what you believe to be right, even if it means a disruption in the visible church. The true church–the invisible church–is still united. This explanation did not satisfy everyone, but it helped justify what looked like a tearing apart of Christ's body and allowed the Reformation to continue.

Early leaders of the Stone-Campbell Restoration Movement turned the Protestant "invisible church" idea upside down. They did believe that the true church was united in the mind of God. But instead of justifying division, they insisted that the fact all true Christians *are* united ought to motivate us to end the scandalous situation and make that unity visible. The strategy proposed by leaders like Stone and the Campbells was to appeal to individual Christians–the faithful scattered throughout "the sects"–to abandon the divisions created by denominationalism and unite on the clear teachings of Scripture. In every locality all those united to Christ would come together to form a church of Christ, inherently one with all other such groups.

The Invisible or Universal Church: A Biblical Concept

And day by day the Lord added to their number those who were being saved.-Acts 2:47

There is one body and one Spirit, just as you were called to the one hope of your calling, one Lord, one faith, one baptism, one God and Father of all, who is above all and through all and in all.

–Ephesians 4:4-6

Our plea of "unity on the clear teachings of Scripture" came partly from Presbyterian restorationist genes and partly from Enlightenment relatives with certain beliefs about human reason that we'll see shortly. Before Stone and the Campbells, most restorationists believed they had to separate completely from the corrupt visible church to be true Christians. In contrast, leaders in the Stone-Campbell Movement believed that a restoration of the clear teachings of Scripture as the terms of Christian fellowship was the only way Christians could be united. This idea became an essential part of the Movement's thought early in the nineteenth century when the religious groups around them were mostly uninterested in unity.

Features Inherited from the Enlightenment Branch of the Family

As we saw in chapter two, the Enlightenment is one of those times in human history when major shifts take place in the way people think about their world and how it works. The Enlightenment ushered in the "modern" era that has shaped us so profoundly. The German philosopher Immanuel Kant (1724-1804) described it as humankind's "emergence from a self-inflicted minority." Minors must rely on someone else to guide them, to tell them what to do and believe. Kant believed that the Christian religion in the form of the institutional church had been that self-appointed guardian for centuries. Both Catholic and Protestant churches, he believed, had kept society from maturing as it should. Kant and others called for humans to "have the courage to make use of your own understanding," throwing off the thought-control of dogmatic church leaders. The Enlightenment's strong emphasis, then, was on human ability–to think, to reason, to come to truth through our God-given mental powers without outside intervention.

In the early years of this shift the English philosopher John Locke (1632-1704) had tremendous influence on the way people understood how one comes to "know" something. In his day many believed that certain truths were innate. Everyone just automatically knew them–they were in everyone's mind from birth. Locke believed, on the other hand, that all knowledge was the result of experiences. The mind, far from being filled with "innate ideas," was a blank slate ready to be written on. Knowledge, therefore, comes through personal experiences of life or having someone transmit their experiences to your "blank slate" through words–teaching. Education became extremely important for those who followed Locke's ideas.

Locke also promoted religious toleration. Though he certainly did not advocate religious indifference, in his "Letter On Toleration" he explained his view that religious bodies were voluntary societies. Their members had chosen to be part of them. If someone chose not to follow the rules of a particular church, they could be excluded from that church–but the matter ended there. The state should never persecute citizens simply for failing to adhere to the rules of a particular religious group. But Locke also insisted that no church should require anything of its members that was not explicitly taught in Scripture as required for salvation. Locke's ideas would become especially influential in the new religious situation of America.

Both Thomas and Alexander Campbell knew Locke's writings well. The "Letter on Toleration" comes through loud and clear all through one of the Movement's founding documents–Thomas Campbell's *Declaration and Address* (1809). Later Alexander Campbell called Locke the "great Christian philosopher" and reprinted large sections of the "Letter on Toleration" in a five-article series in the 1844 *Millennial Harbinger*. Though he apologized for Locke's antiquated style of writing, Campbell asserted that the truths in that short essay were worth more than those in a hundred books of his own day.

Another important piece of our Enlightenment heritage is often

> Whosoever requires those things in order to ecclesiastical communion, which Christ does not require in order to life eternal, he may perhaps indeed constitute a society accommodated to his own opinion and his own advantage; but how that can be called the church of Christ, which is established upon laws that are not his, and which excludes such persons from its communion as he will one day receive into the Kingdom of heaven, I understand not.
>
> –Locke on Toleration, *Millennial Harbinger*, 1844

called the Scottish Common Sense philosophy. Thomas Reid (1710-1796) and Dugald Stewart (1753-1828) developed these ideas during their careers at the University of Glasgow and influenced the thinking of generations of English-speaking people. Simply stated, Reid insisted that people can trust their senses. When you see someone, hear their voice, touch their hand, and so forth, these are not mere illusions produced by your mind as some skeptical philosophers like David Hume (1711-1776) were saying. These sense experiences are true and correspond to reality.

Reid and Stewart taught that, because we can trust our senses, the way people come to know something is by careful observation. In their view there was no room for the imagination in figuring things out. They just wanted the facts, and you got the facts by slow, deliberate, research. They insisted that the proper way to conduct any investigation was to use the inductive method of Sir Francis Bacon. This method started with observing many specific instances of something, then cautiously reasoning from the specifics to a general principle. By this procedure people could discover the laws of nature, or any other truth, and be assured beyond any doubt that they had the facts–free from opinion or speculation. These ideas became extremely influential in early nineteenth-century America, and in the Stone-Campbell Movement. The first college established by our people was named Bacon College after "Lord Bacon." And the application of these ideas to how we arrive at religious truth became normative. You go to the Bible and through a careful, meticulous, rational process, you can discern the facts located there.

We inherited several important Enlightenment features including belief in the individual's ability to come to truth, an emphasis on education, the mandate to require only what the Bible requires, and faith in the reliability of human reason. These were strong traits and in many ways good ones. They have shaped our personality in significant ways for two centuries.

Our American Legacy

These optimistic Enlightenment ideas especially fit the hearty people who came to forge a new life in America. Enlightenment thinkers in the old country had assumed there was a "natural" aristocracy who were best suited to determine the directions for nations and people as opposed to the old notions of hereditary aristocracy and divine right of monarchs. But the Americans took Enlightenment ideas about human reason even farther. The ability to think and reason is not limited to a relatively few extraordinarily gifted people, they insisted. It is the common property of all people–the *common* sense. They completely "democratized" the idea of natural aristocracy. In America–everybody was a natural aristocrat! Ordinary folk, the common people, had just as much access to truth as anyone. In fact, those tainted by theological or other training were often blinded from seeing truths that an ordinary person using common sense could see clearly.

In religion this Americanization of Enlightenment ideas led to the assumption that every individual who approached the Scripture with an honest heart, common sense, and the proper methods would arrive at the *same* truth in all matters of Christian belief and practice. Different conclusions and practices meant that something was wrong in heart, mind, or method. The Reformation had emphasized the Bible as the ultimate source of religious truth and encouraged literacy so every individual could read and know the Bible. Yet in America more than anywhere before, individualism became the chief operating principle. It was not that every individual could come up with his or her own personal truth. Rather every honest individual working separately would arrive at the *same* truth. Truth was one, and all must arrive at that one truth. The reality that equally honest people using the same methods and with equal common sense sometimes arrived at different conclusions led to intense conflict on the American religious scene.

Conclusion

Our family tree is filled with heroes of faith from centuries past. We received a rich inheritance from our Reformation, Enlightenment, and American ancestors. We owe much of our genetic makeup to our Puritan great grandparents, especially the Presbyterians. But we also share significant DNA with our Anabaptist, Arminian, separatist, and independent cousins. We inherited a longing for the unity of the church from our Lutheran and Reformed relatives, and a strong strand of optimism and rationalism from our Enlightenment uncles. And all these features were nurtured in the womb of America.

This is our ancestry. This is partly why we are the people we are–why we "have blue eyes instead of brown." It is not the whole story. God continues to work among his people today to shape them in profound ways if we will let him. But acknowledging our genealogy no more lessens our authenticity as Christians than recognizing inherited traits from physical relatives makes us less than complete people. In fact, we have much to be proud of and much to learn from these fascinating ancestors.

Our early "parents" in the Stone-Campbell Movement struggled to understand God's will in their own time and place. In that struggle they formed a new branch of the family tree. They carried the traits of their ancestors with them, the bloodlines were clear. That is the point of this chapter. Yet this new family faced circumstances that caused them to develop their own unique characteristics. We turn to some of those in the next chapter.

The Shape of Our Family Tree

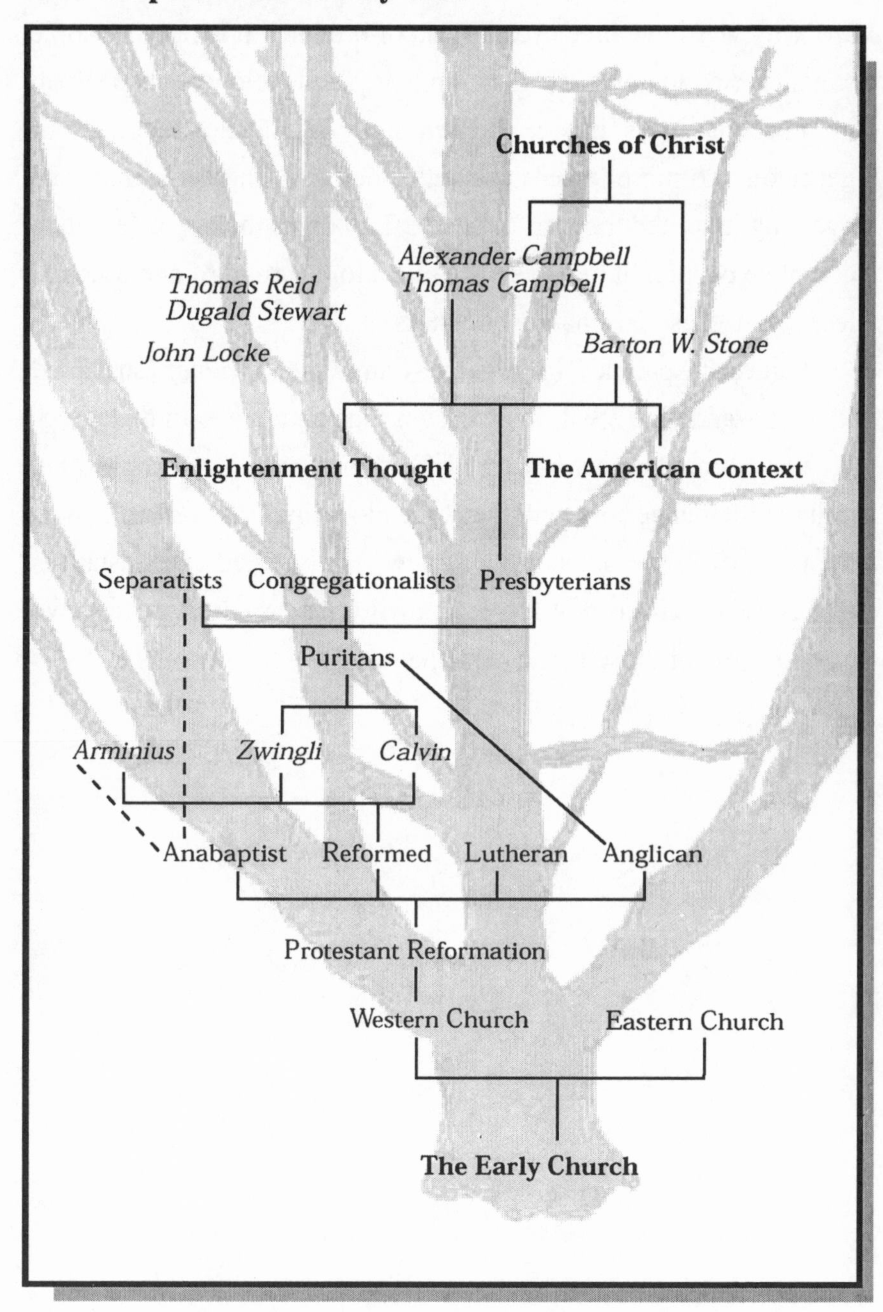

Chapter 5

The Shaping of Our Theology

The process of conversion among the first Christians was a very simple one. It consisted of an utter abandonment of their heathenism, and an entire submission to those new truths which came to them through the revelation of the Gospel, and through it only. It was the pure theology of Christ and his Apostles. That theology which struts in fancied demonstration from a professor's chair, formed no part of it.

–Thomas Chalmers
in the *Christian Baptist*,
October, 1828

Theology. The word does not come easily off our lips. It has an unfamiliar and even unpleasant sound in most of our ears. Growing up in Churches of Christ in the mid-twentieth century, we didn't hear the word "theology" much, not even in our Christian colleges. In fact, for most of the history of our schools, no course even bore the title "theology." Instead of "New Testament Theology," we had "Religious Teachings of the New Testament." What schools in other traditions called "Biblical Theology" we titled "Great Bible Doctrines."

If this reluctance to use the language of theology was true of our colleges, it was certainly true of our churches. If the word was mentioned from the pulpit, it almost always had negative connotations. Theology is what people did in the denominations. It's what led them astray in the first place. Theology was bad because it was human speculation. It was the work of people refusing to rely on God's word, who invented theories about what to believe and practice that resulted in apostasy and division in the church. If they hadn't done all that theology, they would have been simple New Testament Christians. The opposite of doing theology was just going back to the Bible and letting it speak for itself. Theology was not something we wanted to be guilty of!

The problem was in how we understood theology. At its root the term simply means "words about God," thinking about God. It's what people do when they try to understand the profound truths of Christianity. It is a natural and essential Christian activity–in fact, it is unavoidable. Christians are responsible for explaining their faith, for giving an answer to everyone who asks (1 Peter 3:15). The New Testament charges us with the need to grow in knowledge, moving beyond first principles to deeper and more mature understandings (Hebrews 5:13-6:3; Ephesians 4:13). Theology is simply part of who we are.

So how did we get such a bad taste in our mouths for theology? We actually came by this antagonism honestly. Since the earliest days of the church Christian leaders had written descriptions of the faith to instruct believers and non-believers in the basic doctrines of Christianity. They wanted these statements to be true to Scripture and the practice of the apostolic church. At times, though, they found there was no absolutely clear and final teaching on some very important matters–like how Jesus could be both human and divine. They struggled to say something that would build up the church and not compromise truth. In the process they produced insightful statements of faith that have shaped Christian belief ever since.

All theology, whether done by individuals or groups, is tied to its own time, circumstances, and culture. That does not make theology evil. It would be ridiculous to suppose that anyone's beliefs could or ought to be detached from who they are and the circumstances that have shaped them. The problem comes when someone in power tries to impose their theology on all other believers. The Roman government itself, for example, required church leaders in the fourth century to accept the Nicene creed or suffer banishment. Powerful church leaders were always involved too. Centuries later the medieval Inquisition was the logical result of the attitude that everyone must line up with a specific theological formula or be destroyed.

The Protestant churches also eventually explained their beliefs in creeds and confessions. Each denomination held up its statement as the standard of faith. Since they were all different, giving your allegiance to one separated you from Christians in other groups. When the leaders of the Stone-Campbell Movement denounced theology, they were largely denouncing statements of faith imposed by denominational powers that divided Christians. They certainly disagreed with some doctrines taught in those confessions too. But they were not opposed to statements of belief. Thomas Campbell called such efforts "highly expedient," and the more full and explicit the better. But they must never be made terms of communion, he said, because they are based on "human reason"–in other words, they are tied to their own time, circumstances, and culture.

Our early leaders, then, opposed theology in this sense. Yet they were certainly serious about their faith, serious enough to think it through and discuss it thoroughly. As they struggled and studied and thought, they formed strong and clear beliefs about every Christian issue and expressed those beliefs in sermons, tracts, books, and

> We are by no means to be understood as at all wishing to deprive our fellow Christians of any necessary and possible assistance to understand the Scriptures, or come to a distinct and particular knowledge of every truth they contain, for which purpose the Westminister Confession and Catechisms may, with many other excellent performances prove eminently useful.
>
> –Thomas Campbell, *Declaration and Address*

articles. They wrestled with issues like the nature of God, Christ, the church, and humanity–all categories of theology! They sometimes warned their hearers and readers not to create new creeds based on what they were saying. Yet as they worked through issues–usually in public through their articles and debates–many in the Stone-Campbell Movement came to hold those same positions. Even as they denounced theology, they were creating an unacknowledged yet defining theology.

Churches of Christ developed their theology over against the Christian Churches in the fights at the end of the nineteenth century. We stated our beliefs about God, Christ, Scripture, salvation, and the church, especially the church, clearly and passionately. As had been the case with the first generation leaders, we did not count what we were doing as theology–we were simply stating and explaining the clear teachings of Scripture. But we were definitely speaking words about God. Again, despite our protests, we were doing theology, and lots of it.

Enlightenment attitudes about how people gain knowledge led many people to believe that the way *they* thought was simply *the* way to think and know anything. The leaders of the Stone-Campbell Movement were not exempt from such beliefs. They swam in the same intellectual and philosophical stream. They believed that anyone with "common sense" and honesty would be able to see things as they did. This attitude was the natural response to the intellectual and spiritual assumptions of the times, and it was noble in its intent. Nevertheless, as is true in every age, their perspectives were susceptible to certain kinds of arrogance.

Words About the Church–Ecclesiology

At the heart of the Stone-Campbell Movement was a deep concern for the church–both its purity and its unity. Some would say that we in Churches of Christ have made the doctrine of the church the foundation for all our other beliefs. Whether or not this is true, our views on the church have been crucial to our identity. Examining how our spiritual ancestors developed their theology of the church will help us understand something of the crisis we are experiencing today.

The Campbells and Stone were all from Presbyterian backgrounds, heavily influenced by Puritan thought. The Puritans argued that the only way to purify the church was to return to the Bible as the only source of authority. Christians should go to the Scriptures, find the church depicted there, and reform the present church to be an exact reflection of that original, true, apostolic one.

Of all the early pioneers, Alexander Campbell had the most systematic approach to this project of restoring the apostolic church. In 1825 he began in his journal *The Christian Baptist* a series of thirty-two articles titled "A Restoration of the Ancient Order of Things." In these articles Campbell described beliefs and practices of the ancient church that through his study of Scripture he believed had been lost or corrupted. His 1836 book *The Christian System* spelled out many of the practices that became identifying marks of

Churches of Christ. High on the list was congregational autonomy and leadership under the oversight of local elders.

Thomas Campbell detailed the early Movement's key ideas about the nature of the church in his 1809 "Declaration and Address." There he asserted that "the Church of Christ upon earth is essentially, intentionally, and constitutionally one."

> Proposition 1. The Church of Christ on earth is essentially, intentionally, and constitutionally one; consisting of all those in every place that profess their faith in Christ and obedience to him in all things according to the Scriptures, and that manifest the same by their tempers and conduct, and of none else; as none else can be truly and properly called Christians.
>
> *–Thomas Campbell,*
> "Declaration and Address " 1809

To the leaders of the Movement, the most obvious expressions of Christian division were the denominational structures. These structures naturally drew our first fire, and some of the hottest. In the first document of the American Restoration Movement, "The Last Will and Testament of the Springfield Presbytery" (1804), the signers, including Barton Stone, insisted that there was neither precept nor example in the New Testament for organizations as sessions, presbyteries, synods, or assemblies. Later Stone wrote, "We have long been convinced that the sects, as such, can never unite. Every attempt has proved abortive, and must and will fail, till each sect give up its creed as authoritative, its name of distinction, its spirit of party, and feel willing to decrease that Christ may increase."

The only basis for achieving unity was the clear teachings of Scripture–a restoration of the ancient Gospel and order of things. Our Presbyterian ancestors had insisted on the same. Stone and the Campbells drew heavily from Scottish Common Sense assumptions about how to discover those scriptural teachings. And their American democratic beliefs made them insist that every person had the ability to use his or her own reason to arrive at the same truths.

The terms sect and denomination can be defined sociologically and theologically. A sect is a group that separates itself radically from the world and from other believers, seeing itself as the only true church. A denomination is essentially a body with its own distinctive structure and beliefs. Sociologically, a denomination is at home in its culture and sees itself as one of many legitimate churches. Early leaders of the Stone-Campbell Movement often used the terms interchangeably to mean organizations that divide Christians, though at times they referred to us as a denomination.

As in every restoration movement, the question of exactly what to restore became very important. Christians had struggled since the Reformation to describe the "marks of a true church." The answer varied among our early leaders. Alexander Campbell emphasized restoring the facts of the ancient Gospel seen in Scripture. As already mentioned, he spent years on his "Search for the Ancient Order of Things" series in the *Christian Baptist* and spelled out key items in his *Christian System* and *Christianity Restored.* These included: immersion for remission of sins, taking the Lord's Supper every Sunday, local congregational governance by elders, and simple worship with songs reflecting scriptural concepts. He insisted that these were part of the "Christian institution" and could not be changed without severe consequences.

Barton Stone agreed that Scripture was the final authority and source of knowledge in Christianity. Yet Stone insisted that unless the Spirit of Christ characterized one's life, precise doctrine and correct practice were useless. He condemned those of his own movement who were zealous to impose their views of the Bible on

> I blush for my fellows, who hold up the Bible as the bond of union yet make their opinions of it a test of fellowship; who plead for union of all Christians; yet refuse to fellowship with such as dissent from their notions. Vain men! Their zeal is not according to knowledge, nor is their spirit that of Christ. Such antisectarian-sectarians are doing more mischief to the cause, and advancement of truth, the unity of Christians, and the salvation of the world than all the skeptics in the world. In fact, they create skeptics.
>
> -Barton Stone,
> *Christian Messenger*, 1835.

others as the means to unity. Unity will come, he said, only when followers of Christ have the spirit of the Scriptures, including love, peace and forbearance.

These two emphases might be characterized as head vs. heart or facts vs. spirit. In reality they don't exclude each other; yet these two tendencies have provoked conflict throughout the history of Christianity. In our case, Alexander Campbell's rational approach came out on top. His age was, in many ways, thoroughly rational. But it was also characterized by the fervent revivals of the Second Great Awakening. Campbell never believed it was enough merely to have the facts of the Gospel in one's head. Yet he rejected what he saw as the emotional excesses and weaker emphasis on doctrine characteristic of the revivals Stone embraced. Campbell's training, intelligence, and ability to explain and defend his positions were powerfully persuasive to thousands of people, and we have continued largely in the direction he helped chart for the Movement. Ours was a movement short on emotional expression but rich in facts and ideas.

The Unity Movement Experiences Division

If we had restored the church to what it should be, and many of us came to believe we had, our task became to convince believers in other Christian groups of the truth of our positions. We believed all honest and reasonable people would eventually unite on the core truths we taught, though there might be a wide variety of opinions on non-essential matters. We were convinced that restoring the clear teachings of the New Testament as the only terms of communion would surely bring Christian unity.

The fact that the Movement itself suffered a painful division at the turn of the twentieth century and another in mid-century led many to conclude that the concepts of restoration and unity cannot survive together. For many years we understood restoration and unity as complementary, and they seemed to hold together with little problem. However, when we began to realize that denominational structures were not simply going to go away and that some honest followers of Christ could not be convinced of our positions, the two themes as we had understood them began to come apart. When other approaches to Christian unity appeared in the late nineteenth century, the Christian Churches took a different path. They organized themselves for participation in the early ecumenical movement and eventually rejected the notion of restoration. Churches of Christ held tightly to the concept of restoring New Testament doctrine and practice and rejected participation in ecumenical activities.

Issues in the Division

Instrumental Music in Worship	National Conventions
"Located" Preachers	Women's Role
Biblical Criticism	Ecumenical Activity

Methods of Raising Funds other than Sunday Contribution

Missionary Societies and other Para-Church Institutions

Because of these differences and others, Churches of Christ emerged as a separate body over a fifty-year period following the Civil War. Since the Movement had no official structures beyond the congregational level, the issues that provoked the division had to work their way through every congregation. It was a long and painful process, but by the early 1900s Churches of Christ were regrouping and moving ahead in what they believed were the authentic intentions of the founders.

The division significantly shaped our understanding of the church. Many in Churches of Christ concluded that we were the universal church–the only Christians; an idea some second-generation leaders in the Movement had expressed. Our frustration with what we saw as the apostasy of the Christian Churches seemed to push us even more toward that conclusion. In general, members of Churches of Christ believed we were the only Christians through much of the twentieth century.

Not the Only Christians?

Alexander Campbell was certainly not weak on doctrine, including the New Testament teaching on baptism. Yet Campbell always acknowledged the existence of Christians outside the churches he was associated with. In 1837 he printed an article titled "Any Christians Among Protestant Parties?" written in response to a letter from a sister in Lunenburg, Virginia. The letter pointedly asked how to identify a Christian except by the person's obedience to the command to be baptized. Campbell replied that while willful disobedience clearly disqualified a person from being a genuine Christian, he could not condemn those who innocently misunderstood some specific commandment but who showed the image of Christ in their lives.

> How do I know that any one loves my Master but by his obedience to his commandments? I answer, *In no other way*. But mark, I do not substitute obedience to one commandment, for universal or even general obedience. It is the image of Christ the Christian looks for and loves; and this does not consist in being exact in a few items, but in general devotion to the whole truth so far as known. . . . he who infers that none are Christians but the immersed, as greatly errs as he who affirms that none are alive but those of clear and full vision. . . .every [one] who despises any ordinance of Christ, or who is willingly ignorant of it, cannot be a Christian; still I should sin against my own convictions should I teach any one to think that if he mistook the meaning of any institution, while in his soul he desired to know the whole will of God, he must perish forever.
>
> –Alexander Campbell,
> *Christian Baptist*, 1837

In practice the churches of the Campbell Movement insisted on baptism by immersion for membership. Earlier Barton Stone and the churches of his Movement had practiced "open membership." They allowed people who had been baptized as infants to be members of their congregations if they showed evidence of Christian character in their lives. In time, the majority of churches in the Movement came to accept Campbell's "closed membership" position, though many continued to acknowledge the Christian identity of those in other groups who showed the fruit of the Spirit in their lives.

Alexander Campbell's quest to rediscover the precise doctrines and practices of the primitive church became the chief focus for many in the Movement. Campbell himself frequently reminded people that transforming power was in the person of Christ, not in propositions about him. Still, Campbell helped create a vision of the church that put priority on getting doctrines and practices right. Though he never advocated that the restoration process would end with the creation of the perfect church in this world, he created a mentality that led many, especially in Churches of Christ, to assume precisely that–and that they had accomplished that full restoration.

There were always other voices in our churches, however; voices that challenged the arrogance of such an idea. They continued to see the church as God's creation, much larger and more universal than one American-born body. This notion of Christ's church is clearly at the heart of the original ecclesiology of the Stone-Campbell Movement as they struggled to conform to the biblical vision of the one body of Christ that transcends both time and place.

The Church's Worship

For all Christians in all times the church's worship has been one of the most crucial matters of the faith. Worship is the one thing the church does most together. And through the centuries, forms of worship have often distinguished one Christian group from another. Worship has been so important in our own history that we have always demanded we be sure we are doing the things we should, and doing them the right way. Much of Alexander Campbell's work on the "ancient order" focused on worship. In contrast to the older churches around him, and in keeping with the no-frills practical sensibilities of the American frontier, he rejected what he regarded as the showmanship of choirs and organs for simple congregational singing. He taught the weekly memorial observance of the Lord's Supper, the teaching and preaching of the Word, praying from the heart and not from a prayer book, and contributing to the care of the saints and the extension of the Kingdom.

Campbell's ideas about simplicity of worship were not unique to him. Other "free church" traditions like the Baptists and

Mennonites had long emphasized plain services free from pomp and ritual. Yet the specific combination of practices we adopted did make us distinctive. While there were other religious groups that used only *a cappella* music in worship, our opposition to instrumental music became one of the most deeply ingrained pieces of our identity after the Civil War. In our separation from the Christian Churches this one issue came to symbolize all the issues. Whether or not a church used instruments became a litmus test to determine its faithfulness or corruption. Preachers constructed elaborate arguments based on logic and word studies (especially of the Greek word *psallo*) to prove that only *a cappella* worship could be acceptable to God.

Many in Churches of Christ no longer believe that instrumental music in worship is a salvation issue. Some have rejected that position because they reject the mean-spirited sectarianism sometimes connected with it. Others no longer accept the argument from silence–that since the New Testament doesn't authorize it, it is prohibited. Still others have concluded that to attract non-Christians to the Gospel they must use every available resource, including the most appealing music styles. Few have ever examined the reasons for *a cappella* worship without having an axe to grind. Our early leaders were

The Oldest Style of Christian Music Lives On

Other Christian groups that worship *a cappella* include most branches of the Orthodox Churches world wide, the Primitive Baptist Church, the Orthodox Presbyterian Church, many Mennonite groups, other Anabaptist groups like the Amish, and the Plymouth Brethren. Parts of the current worship renewal movement also find *a cappella* praise to be a refreshing alternative in contemporary-styled services.

blind to some of their assumptions. We are no different. As we reexamine this and all other issues, we need to be able to do so with a non-defensive, humble attitude if we are going to promote healthy discussion of the nature of the church and Christian worship.

Words About Human Nature–Anthropology

Reformation thought generally held that humans are fundamentally flawed, depraved, incapable of doing anything good on their own. This was especially true of the Reformed tradition following Calvin. As part of their Presbyterian heritage, Stone and the Campbells reflect parts of this view of human nature. Alexander Campbell, for example, wrote in the *Christian System* in 1839, "...our nature was corrupted by the fall of Adam before it was transmitted to us; and hence that hereditary imbecility to do good, and that proneness to do evil, so universally apparent in all human beings." And yet, the high view of human ability forged by Enlightenment and early American thought resulted in a clash of ideas about human frailty and human ability. Human ability generally won out in our theology.

The Scriptures teach that humans are responsible for their actions, that we can understand and obey God's commands. "Be perfect as your Father in heaven is perfect." Yet they also teach that not one of us is righteous, that all sin and fall short of God's glory. Campbell was clear that this paradox could be resolved only through the power of Christ. Human character could be "perfected" only through the redemption and transformation accomplished by God's Spirit in our lives. Christians have always struggled to maintain a proper balance between our responsibility and our inability, and Churches of Christ have varied in their success.

One of the most distinctive traits of our heritage is the attempt to blend a high view of human nature with a high view of Scripture when most Christian groups hold to one position or the other. This book itself is based on our belief that people can think through issues and change their minds and actions in ways that will bring them more in line with what God wants them to be. If humans are so flawed and helpless and cannot change their lives for the better, this effort would be futile. Yet we have no illusions that what we say here is the final word. We have prayed and struggled and discussed; we have written and disputed and revised. We trust that the work is not in vain. But we know that only through God's blessing can our efforts accomplish anything.

Members of Churches of Christ have tended to see little immediate involvement of God in their lives. Historically there are many reasons for this, including the emphasis on reason we inherited from Alexander Campbell and our rejection of what we saw as the excesses of the Holiness and Pentecostal Movements. In recent years many have hungered for a heightened sense of God's work in their lives. This openness to see God working in every aspect of our daily existence is a needed corrective to our cautious reluctance to attribute any specific event directly to God's work. As in any case of abuse, we need to be on guard against overreaction. This is just one more area where a deep sense of our heritage can help us correct abuses and shield us against unhealthy reactions.

Words About Salvation–Soteriology

One way of organizing theology is into the seven classic categories seen in the insert (p.120), some of which we have treated separately above. But separating theology into these categories distorts its nature. Each category penetrates and shapes the other in complex ways. You can't talk about the church and human nature without talking about salvation. What is it about human nature that makes salvation necessary, and from what exactly do we need to be saved? What does it mean that the church is made up of all the saved? How does one become saved and part of the church? We've already touched on these questions, but before we close this chapter we need to say something more about two more of the most important parts of the theology of the Stone-Campbell Movement and Churches of Christ.

Baptism

Baptism and its connection with salvation and the church became a matter of intense study and discussion very early in the Movement. At the beginning of the nineteenth century one of Barton Stone's colleagues, Robert Marshall, became convinced of the truth of believer's immersion. Stone tried desperately to talk him out of the notion, but instead Marshall ended up convincing Stone. While he was still not entirely sure what to do about baptism, and he says he actually forgot about the issue for several years during the Great Western Revival, Stone stopped baptizing

Seven Classic Categories of Theology

Theology-teachings about God the Father and Creator

Christology-teachings about the person and work of Christ

Pneumatology-teachings about the person and work of the Holy Spirit

Anthropology-teachings about nature and abilities of humankind

Soteriology-teachings about God's work of salvation

Ecclesiology-teachings about the nature and function of church

Eschatology-teachings about the end of time and future life

infants. When he and his fellow ministers began to consider the issue again, they decided that they would be tolerant. Those who had been immersed were not to despise those who had not and vice-versa. Stone later wrote some of the strongest statements to be found anywhere about the biblical teaching of baptism, and most members of his Movement were eventually immersed. Yet the Stone churches continued to have a spirit of tolerance toward those baptized as infants and who were not convinced of the necessity of adult immersion.

As Presbyterians, both Thomas and Alexander Campbell were baptized as infants. Even before coming to America, however, they had been influenced by the thinking of independents who broke with their state churches and began baptizing only adult believers. The subject came up in discussions several times in the early years of their work, but it was the birth of Alexander Campbell's daughter in 1812 that motivated him finally to study the matter in depth. He concluded that he could not baptize his infant daughter, and, furthermore, since he had been baptized as an infant, he needed to submit to biblical baptism.

Campbell continued to expand his knowledge of baptism as he studied, wrote, and debated. Yet from this time on he vigorously taught the immersion of penitent believers as the baptism of the New Testament. When he wrote his book of theology, the *Christian System*, he spent more time by far on baptism than any other subject.

No responsible teacher in the Movement ever taught "baptismal regeneration," that there is something magic in the act itself. God saves us by grace through our faith in Jesus Christ. But it is in the act of submission to Christ's command to be baptized that God gives us His grace and salvation. Our teaching of baptism was different from that of all the other churches. Like the Baptists we believed that the only proper subjects for baptism were penitent believers and that biblical baptism was immersion. Unlike the Baptists and like many Protestants, Catholics, and Orthodox, we believed that God acted in baptism to (among other things) forgive sins and move one from the Kingdom of darkness to the Kingdom of light. This was and has continued to be an essential belief for Churches of Christ.

The question was, how were we to regard those who had been baptized as infants, but who professed their faith in Christ and showed it in lives marked by the fruit of the Spirit. Both Stone and Campbell, as soon as they were convinced of the biblical teaching, eagerly submitted to immersion. They taught and practiced it for the rest of their lives. After the first generation it was rare for an unimmersed person to be part of one of the churches of the Stone-Campbell Movement. Yet we've already seen how Campbell responded to the woman from Lunenburg, Virginia. He stated in no uncertain terms, "I cannot make any one duty the standard of Christian state or character, not even immersion into the name of the Father, of the Son, and of the Holy Spirit and in my heart regard all that have been sprinkled in infancy without their own knowledge and consent as aliens from Christ and the well-grounded hope of heaven."

Some accused Campbell of giving up his convictions on baptism and damaging the Movement with this statement. He denied it and stated again his convictions regarding biblical baptism. The plea had always been that Christians should come out of the divisive denominations and unite on the simple Gospel. If there were no

Australian Churches of Christ and Baptism

In a recent booklet, written by Australian Gordon Stirling, titled *Churches of Christ: Reinterpreting Ourselves for the New Century*, the author reflects on how the "Associated" Churches of Christ in that nation have wrestled with the issue of baptism. Tracing their history to the mid-1800s when Scotch Baptists and British restorationists immigrated to Australia, these churches have always emphasized the importance of New Testament baptism.

Many of their churches and leaders, however, have participated in ecumenical activities with unimmersed people. Because of this, some have accused these churches of abandoning the teaching and practice of immersion. That is not the case. Stirling is adamant that immersion is an essential part of the life of Australian Churches of Christ.

> *It is not an optional extra. While we accept as fellow Christians all for whom Christ is Lord and Saviour, whether their understanding of baptism is different from ours or not, we have a commitment to witness to what we are convinced is valid biblical baptism. And while we accept that God honours the intentions of godly parents who bring their children for infant baptism and commit themselves to bringing them up "in the nurture and admonition of the Lord," . . . we cannot accept infant baptism as being biblical. Infant baptism is a commitment made on behalf of another, whereas Christian commitment can only be the result of a conscious personal decision. We can worship, serve, study, socialise and witness with those whose understanding of baptism is different from ours, . . . but we are committed to witnessing to the fact that biblical baptism is the immersion of penitent believers. This commitment is not only for our conscience's sake, but for the sake of the whole Christian church.*

Christians in the denominations, the plea would make no sense. He stated repeatedly that he believed if a person rejected or intentionally neglected immersion, that person could not be a Christian. But if we accused people of being rebels against God because they took it for granted that had been scripturally baptized–when their lives were filled with love and active benevolence, they were faithful in worship and taught their family the fear of the Lord, when their constant companion was the Bible–then it was the accuser who was in error.

This issue has been crucial for us since the earliest days. At times we have been extremely sectarian by effectively denying that anyone outside our churches could be a true Christian because we were the only ones who taught and practiced the biblical doctrine of baptism. At other times we have admitted that there might be Christians in other groups, though there was little or no practical application of the idea. A few may have downplayed our strong teaching on immersion of believers to be able to cooperate with people from other religious bodies.

We are convinced that we must not dilute our insistence on New Testament baptism. But we are also convinced that we cannot allow our resolute stance on this issue to keep us isolated from the kinds of godly people Campbell described in his articles on baptism.

Many in Churches of Christ have rejected opportunities to participate in activities with believers in other churches because they believed it would lead to compromise and abandonment of the truths we have held so strongly–especially baptism. The truth is that in cooperative efforts and theological conversations, if those who come to the table don't bring something of substance, if they cannot explain their beliefs in a way that is clear and convincing, they have no reason to be there. Involvement in such efforts does not require that people compromise their beliefs to be part of the conversation. In fact, it usually forces participants to reexamine and strengthen their convictions.

Baptism is a live issue in the Christian world today. Being open to hear the views of others will allow us to have a hearing as well. Churches of Christ have a strong reason to be present in the conversation. In a real sense we are, in Gordon Stirling's words, "the guardians of certain truths and values without which the whole church would be poorer." We too will benefit from insights and understandings of other groups who because of their own circumstances have emphasized other truths.

Regardless of what some have accused us of in the past, Churches of Christ need to emphasize, explore, and teach more about baptism, not less. But we cannot do it in an isolated, abrasive, and sectarian manner as we sometimes have.

Scripture

We close this brief historical look at some of our most important theological traits with a word about our view of Scripture. Since we will examine this topic in chapter seven and in an entire volume later in this series, we will say only a few things here. Like most Protestants, our early leaders emphasized Scripture as the final authority in religion and the only legitimate source of our beliefs and practices. However, while most groups relied also on written creeds and confessions to give their official interpretation of Scripture, we rejected all such statements. One of our early slogans, "No creed but the Bible," reflected our belief that divisive creeds and the theology that produced them were the enemies of a restoration of biblical Christianity and Christian unity. Thomas Campbell formulated another key slogan that embodied our seriousness about Scripture as guide: "Where the Scriptures speak we speak, and where the Scriptures are silent we are silent."

Both these slogans indicated our intention to be faithful to Scripture and to Scripture alone in all we said and did. Slogans, however, are highly abbreviated, usually oversimplified, and open to different understandings. Some took the first one, "no creed but the Bible," to mean that we were not to interpret the Bible but simply to let it speak for itself. They seemed not to realize that they were engaging the Scripture, using their minds to make sense out of it, and applying it to their lives. In other words, they were interpreting it!

Speaking where the Bible speaks seems easy enough to understand, but being silent where it is silent meant different things to different people from the very first. Some saw it as restricting–if the Bible doesn't say to do it, we can't do it. Others saw it as freeing–if the Bible doesn't mention something, we can use our own judgment, being careful not to violate any clear principle or impose our judgment on others. These varying understandings were not new with the Stone-Campbell Movement. As we saw in chapter four, Reformation leaders Martin Luther and Ulrich Zwingli disagreed sharply over the very same issue. The restrictive idea eventually led groups like the Amish and Mennonites to refuse any "unscriptural" practices, including the use of automobiles and buttons. Differences over the silence of Scripture were extremely important in the division between the Churches of Christ and the Christian Churches. The issue of silence continued to be troublesome in the twentieth century as we debated questions like whether or not to have Sunday

Schools. We generally took the position that silence restricts, though we have found it difficult to apply uniformly.

Members of Churches of Christ in the nineteenth and early twentieth centuries framed their questions and arrived at answers based on their experiences and the assumptions they had about the Bible and Christianity. On the surface there is nothing surprising about that–it is stating the obvious. But we have operated so often as if we were immune from the influence of events and unstated assumptions that we need to state the obvious, and state it often. The questions we were asking and the way we were asking them assumed that the Bible functions essentially as a rule book. This assumption was so widely held, it often went unstated. It led inevitably to an approach that emphasized our duty to mine, collect, and organize the laws and commands embedded in Scripture. As we will see in chapter seven, this is not the only way to approach Scripture, nor is it the best. Our theology with its strengths and its weaknesses looks the way it does partly because of this approach.

Conclusion

There is much more to the theology of Churches of Christ than what we have touched on in this chapter. We have not even mentioned specifically all of our "distinctives." What this chapter (along with the previous one) intended to convey, however, is that we do have a theology, and this theology has a context–a long and rich history that stretches back even beyond our American origins two hundred years ago. We are convinced that much of that theology is solid, healthy and true. We also know that our conclusions are the product of imperfect human struggles to please God in specific circumstances. While truth does not change, our understanding of truth must constantly undergo scrutiny and rethinking. In some of our conclusions we may have been influenced more by the circumstances of our times than by the Spirit of Christ, and in those cases scrutiny and rethinking with humility can bring us closer to what God wants us to be. We turn now to an examination of the specifics of our current crisis.

Chapter 6

Our Current Crisis

Above all guard your heart, for it is the wellspring of life.
Put away perversity from your mouth; keep corrupt talk far from your lips.
Let your eyes look straight ahead, fix your eyes directly before you.
Make level paths for your feet and take only ways that are firm.
Do not swerve to the right or the left; keep your foot from evil.

–Proverbs 4:23-27

Crisis is one of those words you just don't want to hear. It means that things are seriously *not* what they should be. It means that the normal way of doing things has been disrupted and priorities rearranged. It means that things you cherish are in danger, maybe even your whole way of life. A crisis is something people will do almost anything to end. If a crisis continues for long, people become increasingly fearful, frantic, and even destructive. The nuclear crisis, the Middle East crisis, the Gulf War crisis, all conjure up images of terrible danger and the need for quick and extreme measures to get things right again. When individuals, families, or nations are suddenly faced with circumstances that threaten their well being and even existence, they are in crisis.

We're certainly not the first to say that Churches of Christ are in crisis. Hundreds of people have written millions of words in recent decades trying to describe and remedy our predicament. We can take little comfort in the realization that we are not alone in this, that every other religious body is experiencing similar pressures. We have to deal with our own state of affairs. Once we had a strong sense of our identity. We sang the same songs, used the same Bible school literature, read the same papers and knew the same "big" preachers. Through articles, sermons, and lectures we at least knew what the accepted positions were on most doctrinal issues.

That sense of stability and certainty from the early and middle years of the twentieth century is largely gone. Our papers have polarized, lectureships attract increasingly narrow audiences, and preachers who are influential in one segment of the churches are often unknown or demonized in others. While there is still an amazing consensus on many teachings and practices, you can never be sure about what you're going to get when you visit a congregation in another place. Today our churches reflect a wide range of positions on all the issues. Some are threatened by what they see as an abandonment of our core identity, a tossing aside of the good and true things that have made us who we are. Others believe that the real danger to our existence is in holding blindly to ways of the past. Our traditionalism, they insist, is preventing us from being relevant to a culture desperately in need of relevant Christianity. We are in crisis.

The Shaping of Our Identity

As we have seen, events of the late nineteenth and early twentieth centuries were crucial in shaping the identity of Churches of Christ as an identifiable body. Two things in particular affected how we understood ourselves: the ideas of restoration and unity we inherited from the early Movement, and the bitter division between the Christian Churches and us. Of course, one reason the divisive fights developed in the first place was that different people had conflicting notions about what restoration and unity meant. As the conflict progressed and people took sides, we were increasingly convinced that we were the ones who had preserved the original ideals of the Movement. Those who took positions different from ours had abandoned the cause and were clearly unfaithful digressives and apostates.

Those battles in the first division of the Stone-Campbell Movement profoundly shaped our identity. Churches of Christ emerged from that crisis emphasizing certain teachings and practices over others. If the burning issues of the time had been the nature of the Lord's Supper or the ordination of ministers instead of instrumental music in worship and missionary societies, we would have come out with a different identity. Please don't misunderstand; all of these matters are important for Christians to deal with. Nevertheless, the fact is that the issues that became the marks of Churches of Christ became so not because they are the most prominent topics in Scripture, but because of what happened to us in the nineteenth and twentieth centuries.

In 1979, Joe Barnett published a widely circulated tract titled "The Churches of Christ: Who Are These People?" Aimed at a religious audience unfamiliar with us and our positions, Barnett discussed what he saw as our key identifying traits. His list is a helpful summary of key characteristics of Churches of Christ. After some membership figures, Barnett provided a brief description of our ideal of restoring the New Testament church, including rejection of creeds and denominational divisions. He then listed the following features that make us who we are: self-governing congregations with elders and deacons; five items of worship–singing, praying, preaching, giving, and the Lord's Supper; *a cappella* singing in worship; the Lord's Supper every Sunday; the five-step plan of salvation–hear, believe, repent, confess, be baptized; and the practice of believer's immersion for the remission of sins.

Many religious people looking at this list would surely think it odd that some extremely important items have been left out and some fairly secondary ones included. Why doesn't he mention that we believe in the divinity of Christ and the inspiration and authority of Scripture? Why aren't our beliefs in one God and the second coming of Christ listed? Barnett omitted such weighty Christian doctrines not because he judged them to be less important than the things he includes, but because he took it for granted that his readers would know we believed them. He was saying, in essence, here are the things that set us apart. These beliefs and practices together make us different from others who claim to be Christians and give us a unique identity in the maze of Christian bodies that exists today.

Fear of Losing What is Important

Yes, Barnett's list is limited. But no accurate list could leave out the things he includes. And it would be unlikely that a congregation could change any one of those characteristics significantly and still be regarded as part of the fellowship of Churches of Christ. It should come as no surprise, then, when members of our congregations who have always held these things raise an alarm when they believe some among us are abandoning them.

Those who fear losing these teachings and practices point out that these are the very issues we have defended most vigorously through the years against our religious neighbors and the "digressives" in our midst. These are points of doctrine that have been the frequent subject of sermons and lessons, defended vigorously with Scripture and logic. Giving in on these matters would be nothing short of the most vile betrayal, they believe. If these things were true once, they must be true always because God's will does not change. For many in Churches of Christ the crisis is precisely this. Misguided or perverse "change agents" are forsaking "the things surely believed among us" and are leading others to forsake them as well. In the process they are threatening to destroy Christ's church.

Often those who see our crisis as one of forsaking key teachings have the same attitude as the "true Lutherans" mentioned in chapter four. Those leaders believed that every doctrinal conclusion they reached, regardless of whether it was central or on the fringe, had to be defended equally as part of the package. Today no one in Churches of Christ would deny that some doctrines are closer to the center of Christian life and thought than others. Certainly baptism is more important than having elders, for example. Many congregations have functioned for years without elders, but no congregation could dispense with or minimize baptism for long without being regarded as outside the fellowship of Churches of Christ. The point is, like the "true Lutherans" we have insisted that our positions were the true ones–all of them. Others would have to come around to the same conclusions to be saved.

Our identity is defined, though, by our theological positions and practices *and* our attitude toward others. Though it's painful to admit, our exclusive attitude may be the character trait most widely known among outsiders. "Oh, they're the folks who think they're the only ones going to heaven." While there were always leaders among us who fought such sectarianism, much of our literature through the twentieth century reflects precisely that belief. It grew out of the conviction that we had restored the New Testament church in its fullness–at least in the areas that really counted–and that anyone who claimed to follow Christ but refused to come to our positions was not really a Christian at all.

Today many are fearful that if we abandon the understanding of ourselves as at least the most perfect Christians–if not the only ones–we would be abandoning our very identity as Christians. To admit that there are others as eager to please God and follow Christ as we are and who are doing so out of their own historical context with its strengths and weaknesses, seems to be an admission that we don't deserve to exist. If we are not right in our positions, some insist, we ought to close the doors and go where they are right. Giving it all up is, of course, unthinkable, so the only possible course of action is to continue to insist that we are the only Christians.

The idea that we are the only Christians assumes at least two things: (1) that being right in every belief and practice is the only legitimate reason for the existence of Churches of Christ, and (2) that we cannot admit the true Christian identity of believers in other groups without forfeiting our reason for being. Neither of these assumptions is true. We certainly are responsible for serious study of God's word, for searching out and understanding his will revealed in Scripture. Furthermore, we can and must know God's will and follow it with his help.

But no human or group of humans can ever be perfect in their understandings. Nothing could be clearer in Scripture than the truth that our salvation ultimately depends on what God has done, not on what we do. For true Christians, realizing these facts could never lead to an attitude of complacency–that there's no use even trying since we can't get it all right, and God will take care of it anyway. Just the opposite! For those who love God and want to know and do God's will, admitting imperfection and reliance on God's work can only lead to a lifetime of diligent study, maturing understanding, and humble service. We are safe in His hands, and we continue to grow, but in this life we will never reach a stopping point in purity or knowledge.

Once Churches of Christ came to believe that we had completely restored the ancient church, and once we saw that not all those who claimed to follow Christ were going to come over to our way of thinking, Churches of Christ became increasingly isolated. It was natural to conclude that we were the only Christians. A statement made in the 1940 Abilene Christian College Bible lectures was the overwhelmingly typical attitude. "If we are too weak-kneed and yellow-livered to tell those in denominational institutions that they are lost and there is only one divine institution, namely the church of Christ, I fear for us in the day of judgment."

As we saw in chapter five, however, this was not the attitude of the founding leaders of the Movement. Please understand, no one is claiming perfection for those early leaders. What we are saying is that our "reason for being" does not depend on the claim that we are the only Christians. We came into existence without any such claim and have continued to exist in three centuries without the necessity

We're Not the Only Christians

I presume that we are all agreed that our church, or our people, are a part or portion of the "Church of Christ." I believe more than this that all other bodies of professing Christians, who accept Christ as the Saviour and Redeemer, are also parts and portions of the "Church of Christ." I am constrained to believe thus when I remember that "Christ's Church" has existed and been in full and active operation since the day of Pentecost, and consequently long before our people were ever known or heard of...I fear we do not rejoice as much as we should when we hear of conversions to Christ in other denominations–and yet we should do so, without one shade of envy or regret that they did not join our own body.

–*Millennial Harbinger*, September 1870

We Are the Only Christians

If we as a body cannot prove our identity with the Christian church of apostolic days; if we originated long after this; and if our conditions are not the law of the New (Christian) Institution delivered by the Holy Spirit through inspired men, then let us hasten to shuffle off the unchristian coil, immolate it on the funeral pyre, and having consumed the unholy form, let us henceforth seek a purer, a higher and a more Christlike existence. But . . . if we are ready at all times to repudiate all that is shown to be merely human, and to accept all that is Divine, then we are in no sense a denomination or sect,–a division from nor in the Body of Christ–but the glorious body itself, ruled and directed by its Divine Head.

–*Millennial Harbinger*, October 1870

We're Not the Only Christians

The issue is not whether a group of disciples has the right to claim to be Christians only. Rather, it is whether those who are "Christians only" can justifiably profess to be the only Christians and that all others are thereby outside the borders of the Kingdom of God. The boundaries of the Kingdom encompass all who have been born into the divine family . . . . Only God can expunge their names from the book of life. For us to exclude them because we perceive some error in their thinking or practice is to be guilty of sectarian judgmentalism.

–*Is Christ Divided?*, 1992.

We Are the Only Christians

From the perspective of the world, the church of Christ is a denomination. They see a group that is independent from other groups, so they assume it is merely another of the groups in the denominational system. It is true, of course, that the church of Christ is a separate people; but the church of Christ is not a division of the body of Christ. **It is the body of Christ**. Those who are uninformed may not understand this, and are in need of teaching and study.

–*Carolina Christian*, April 1990.

of it. One of the defining slogans we used in both the nineteenth and twentieth centuries reflected our desire to be "Christians only, but not the only Christians."

Our reason for being is to pursue the goal of growing up into Christ (Ephesians 4:14-15). It is to take the message of the hope of Jesus Christ to those without hope. It is to embody Christ the healer to a sick world. We need no other justification for our existence. We have been gifted with a unique heritage and set of insights. We must not shirk our God-given responsibilities or neglect our God-given gifts by isolating ourselves from other followers of Christ and justifying it as being faithful to our identity.

Fear of Being Weighted Down by Too Much Baggage

On the other hand, some feel that any effort to explain and defend our distinctive beliefs to others will hinder us from representing Christ to the world of the twenty-first century. A few are openly antagonistic to our traditional positions, sometimes because of abuse suffered at the hands of church leaders acting out of our worst sectarian attitudes. Others are not particularly antagonistic, but regard our distinctive beliefs as unnecessary baggage they can easily leave behind as circumstances demand. To these people, the current crisis in Churches of Christ is one of traditionalist leaders who insist on maintaining the old ways and who resist changes that would make us more relevant to our culture. These "traditionalists," they believe, are the real threat to the integrity of Churches of Christ.

Chapter three described the problem suffered by both ultra-traditionalists and anti-traditionalists–they have missed the foundational importance of history and tradition. Anti-traditionalists scorn their heritage in direct attacks and ridicule. Ultra-traditionalists don't believe the teachings they defend *are* traditions. Neither extreme sees the dangers of their attitude because they lack a historical consciousness. As a result both sides ironically are in bondage to the traditions they so despise.

The Literature of Crisis

This is not the first time Churches of Christ have faced crisis. In a very real sense, the Stone-Campbell Restoration Movement was born in crisis. Christians in both America and Europe, partly because of new intellectual, political and social developments, began to question the creeds and structures of the older systems of Christianity. Many rebelled against what they saw as divisive sectarian systems. It was a terrible crisis for the established churches, and when the United States actually prohibited national support for any church in the First Amendment to the Constitution, some thought it was the end of organized religion in America. In reality, the Stone-Campbell Restoration Movement was a big part of the crisis in early American Christianity.

Churches of Christ have faced other major crises in their own history. The division at the turn of the twentieth century changed the way Churches of Christ saw themselves. In the following decades we struggled to find ways to relate to each other when we didn't see eye to eye on doctrines about Christ's second coming. Later we fought over whether we could use para-church institutions to help us carry out Kingdom work. We battled over whether we could participate with other religious groups in moral crusades like the Civil Rights Movement. Crisis is not new. But *this* crisis is.

We've already seen that the alarms today come from a variety of places. Different people see different enemies and suggest very different solutions. In the last part of the twentieth century a huge amount of literature attempted to identify the source of our problems and suggest solutions for the future of Churches of Christ. This "literature of crisis" began to appear in the 1960s with such publications as *Axe on the Root* by Ira Y. Rice, Jr. (3 vols, 1966, 1967, 1970), *Voices of Concern: Critical Studies in Church of Christism* edited by Robert Meyers (1966), a new journal named *Mission* begun in Abilene, Texas in 1967, and the writings of Carl Ketcherside and Leroy Garrett in their respective journals *Mission Messenger* and *Restoration Review*. These writings cover the spectrum from ultra-traditionalist to anti-traditionalist. Still, the main body of churches then was not as fragmented as it would become in the last two decades of the century.

In 1984 another book was especially influential in further defining the crisis. That year *20th Century Christian* published Rubel Shelly's *I Just Want to be a Christian* in which he openly rejected the idea that members of Churches of Christ were the only Christians. Instead he made a strong case for the historic Restoration plea that we can be "Christians only" without denying the Christianity of believers in other groups. Since Shelly had previously been a strong defender of the exclusive idea, his new attitude was a blow to many of his former colleagues. Shelly's book introduced many in Churches of Christ to their heritage of Christian unity and the Stone-Campbell Movement's understandings of the nature of the church. It also heightened the sense of alarm and crisis that had been building for two decades.

Before we proceed, let us issue one word of caution. While labels may be useful to define and contrast positions, they are never entirely accurate. In the 1990s several attempted to put descriptive names on the different positions developing in Churches of Christ. Douglas Foster in *Will the Cycle Be Unbroken* identified six groups he named progressives, pietists, evangelicals, neo-conservatives, fundamentalists, and moderates. The terms covered a lot of ground but needed explanation and still missed important categories. Michael Weed and Gary Holloway tried their hand at describing the main groups in a paper presented in 1995 to Stone-Campbell historians at the Disciples of Christ Historical Society. They describe three "options" taking shape in Churches of Christ: conservative reactionaries, pragmatic change agents, and moderates/neo-conservatives. Still another attempt to capture our current configurations was done by Joe Beam in a 1996 *Wineskins* article titled "What is Happening to Us?" Beam used a traditional left to right chart that labeled individuals as exasperated, open, cautious, searching, satisfied, and zealots. He also labeled churches as left-wing, innovative, traditional, and right-wing.

All of these efforts are insightful. But no scheme or chart can include all the complexities of the way things really are, and inevitably some people and churches get forced into categories that distort their views. The following survey of literature, therefore, will not try to identify and label every possible position. Instead we have organized the material to reflect a spectrum from those who define the crisis primarily as an abandonment of our traditional stances to those who believe we must be less rigid about our traditional stances to meet the needs of the current culture. Let's look at a sampling of this literature from the 1990s.

A Crisis of Abandonment

Two of the more outspoken books of the last decade are William Woodson's *Change Agents and Churches of Christ* and Dave Miller's *Piloting the Straight*. In Woodson's 1994 volume he identifies by name leaders in Churches of Christ who he considers to be dangerous agents of change who are threatening the faithfulness and identity of Churches of Christ. He starts by comparing the change agents to "prattling schoolboys" who don't pose a real threat. He warns, however, that the change-agent movement is parasitic. It doesn't start new churches; instead it latches onto peaceful ones and disrupts them. Woodson accuses change agents of despising the church even as they claim to be its deliverers. He ridicules them for making the claim that they have discovered truths that everyone else before them had missed.

> Our background and commitment is to the Church of Christ that was born of the American Restoration Movement. Our goal is to move that group closer to the church of Christ revealed in Scripture.
>
> –Original *Wineskins* "Statement of Purpose"

Woodson attacks numerous doctrinal errors he believes the change agents are promoting among the churches. Among them are subjective methods of Bible interpretation, the devaluing of baptism as essential to salvation, the restyling of our worship services, the attempt to define a core of essential doctrines, and a new view of grace that covers doctrinal error as well as moral sin. But for Woodson, the one essential error that permeates all the others is the change agents' agenda to define the "church of Christ" as just another denomination among denominations. Referring to the purpose statement of *Wineskins* magazine,

Woodson accuses change agents of redefining the church. No longer is it all those who have been saved by the power of God, but a "man made church that is removed some distance from the church revealed in Scripture." He concludes that while the danger from these change agents is real, resistance to their agenda is growing, and that if these people and their allies refuse to repent and stop, "It is time for them to go."

In the 1996 volume *Piloting the Strait: A Guidebook for Assessing Change in Churches of Christ*, Dave Miller discusses in six lengthy sections a range of issues he believes put Churches of Christ in danger of apostasy. He points to American culture as containing the roots of the current changes, fueled by an attitude of rebellion, a loss of respect for lawful authority, a misunderstanding of restoration, and the corrupting influence of higher education. The mechanism for change, according to Miller, is the "new hermeneutic." This new way of understanding Scripture rejects our traditional method of interpreting Scripture that focuses on command, example, and necessary inference–which he restyles direct statement, accounts of action, and implication. Miller attacks "new hermeneutical" attempts to define a core Gospel and claims the approach is contrary to simple logic. Such an effort is, he says, "simply a ploy–a mechanism–by which those desiring change in the church may achieve their objectives."

Much of Miller's analysis of specific changes focuses on worship practices. He condemns lifting hands, the use of solos and choral groups, clapping, the use of worship teams, and changes in auditorium lighting. Those who do such things are, in Miller's view, showing a spirit of rebellion, insisting on change for its own sake and willing to divide churches to get what they want. In addition he raises alarms over the use of small groups, "Children's Worship," and services dedicating children to God, among many other things.

Miller tackles several other issues that have been particularly troublesome in many of our congregations. He defines adultery exclusively as sexual unfaithfulness and insists that persons coming to Christ who are divorced and remarried for any other reason must leave their current spouses in order to be saved. He rejects any expansion of leadership roles for women, including service as deacons. And he laments the "widespread conspiracy" to blur the differences between the church of Christ and "the spurious counterfeits constructed by men, i.e., the denominations." He labels fraternization with denominations as traitorous–the most sinister, destructive, and tragic of all the changes being made.

In the final sections of his book Miller asserts that the change agents are motivated entirely by pride and a desire for popularity, possessions, and freedom from restraint. In answering the question, "What are the Faithful to Do?" Miller urges his readers to take a middle road between doctrinal conservatives who lack the spirit of Christ, and the unbiblically permissive change agents he has described in the book. In the end though, he urges leaders to identify the change agents, insist on their repentance and cessation, and if they refuse, to expel them.

A more moderate approach, though still very conservative, is the 1998 volume, *Directions for the Road Ahead: Stability in Change Among Churches of Christ.* Edited by Jim Sheerer and Charles L. Williams with essays from sixteen church leaders, the tone of the book is set in the Preface by Howard Norton. Its purpose, he states, is "to clarify and restate some distinctive biblical concepts" that Churches of Christ since their beginning have attempted to restore because these teachings are in danger of being compromised or forgotten. He lists four reasons for concern: (1) these Restoration themes began to be de-emphasized in the 1960s in an over-reaction to our neglect of other important Christian teachings; (2) many in Churches of Christ see these doctrines as embarrassing baggage that separates them needlessly from other conservative Christians; (3) these teachings have not been expressed well in contemporary terms; and (4) the tremendous pressure to change the church has caused many members to question practically all our traditional stances, making an articulate defense of them crucial. We are never more than one generation away from apostasy, Norton warns.

Norton cautions that the essays are not meant to form a creed, nor does each author necessarily agree with all the positions stated by the others. However, he contends that the positions expressed in each essay are the ones held by the Restoration Movement through the years "because they are based firmly on the teachings of Jesus Christ and the inspired apostles." In a chapter on hermeneutics Furman Kearley strongly defends the propositions that the Bible can be understood by all people alike, that the silence of Scripture is binding, and that necessary inference is an important part of interpreting the Bible. Nancy Ferguson argues that women are restricted from any authoritative leadership role in the church's assemblies. Milo Hadwin affirms that the New Testament condemns the use of instrumental music in worship.

Other essays treat New Testament baptism, the inerrancy of Scripture, Church Growth, the work of the Holy Spirit, undenominational Christianity, and the boundaries of fellowship. In contrast to the previous volumes, change is not cast in a totally negative light. In the book's Introduction Jack Lewis contends that if change means understanding truths not adequately understood before, or dropping practices not supported by Scripture, or putting into practice duties that had been neglected, then all truth-loving people should advocate change. The authors generally admit that change is inevitable; yet the tone of the book is very cautious. It provides few tools for dealing with change other than to defend the traditional stances of Churches of Christ–which it does well.

A Crisis of Restrictive Traditionalism

While William Woodson and Dave Miller warn readers that destructive change agents are afoot in the church, and Howard Norton reminds us that we are never more than one generation away from apostasy, Lynn Anderson in his 1994 volume *Navigating the Winds of Change* sounds a very different note. He is not naive about the potential damage these winds can produce, but he mourns the fact that for many the dream of a growing church relevant to the needs of its age has been destroyed by widespread apathy and rigid traditionalism. Anderson believes that along with the chill winds of change are blowing the mighty winds of renewal. He sees a spirit of hope rather than fear dominating many of our congregations and suggests concrete ways for leaders to manage change in their churches in a healthy and biblical way.

Like the others, Anderson focuses much of his attention on worship practices. In contrast to the others, however, he insists that major changes are overdue in our worship styles. "Antiquated, rural styles of worship and religious communication are as foreign to young people of urban, contemporary America as is English spoken in Russia," he contends. He explains the differences between right-brained and left-brained people, the first tending toward the emotional and the second toward the rational. Our traditional worship styles have been predominantly left-brained, while current trends in worship renewal are overwhelmingly right-brained and emotive. This has set us up, Anderson believes, for major clashes as we have introduced new songs, worship orders, and approaches to worship from the worship renewal movement.

Anderson asserts that we must honor those who have gone before us, those who sacrificed to preach the Gospel and build up our churches. But it does not honor them to insist on holding to the forms and methods they used if those forms and methods do not reach the unchurched of our own day. Those early leaders were highly successful in using appropriate strategies for reaching the people of their own time and culture. We show them true respect by doing the same. This means that we will have to know our time and culture well and be willing constantly to evaluate the forms we use to reach them.

Anderson is obviously a "change agent"–an advocate of what he believes is positive change in light of Scripture and our heritage. He does not spend time defending our traditional teachings, and the criticisms he makes are directed primarily at those who resist the changes he advocates in concept and style of worship. Though he admits that the Bible itself fits both "right-brained" and "left-brained" styles, his sentiments are clearly on the side of the right-brained emotive. In the end he outlines strategies for conversation between advocates of healthy change and those who fear change. He concludes with the admonition that only with the attitude described by Paul in Philippians 2:1-4 can healthy change take place. "Do nothing out of selfish ambition or vain conceit."

As mentioned, Douglas Foster attempted to address our current problems in the 1994 book *Will the Cycle Be Unbroken? Churches of Christ Face the Twenty-First Century.* The "cycle" of the title is the one religious sociologists use to describe the life of religious movements. After a vibrant beginning and a period of growth and consolidation, most groups enter a crisis phase where they either divide, die, or are revitalized. Acknowledging that Churches of Christ are in the crisis stage, Foster spends considerable time examining the ways we understand ourselves, including the contradictory views that we are a movement within the universal church and that we *are* the universal church.

Foster lists twenty issues threatening to disrupt Churches of Christ at some level. A few, such as church gymnasiums and the use of "modern" translations of the Bible, are issues to only a very small minority. The majority of the matters, however, are the same ones mentioned in other volumes: biblical hermeneutics, women's role, divorce and remarriage, the work of the Holy Spirit, the nature of worship, and the question of who is a Christian. Yet the point of *Will the Cycle Be Unbroken?* is not to argue the issues. It is to urge an attitude of love and unity. Foster cites the example of T. B. Larimore in the Movement's first division. Despite his high profile ministry Larimore refused to be pushed into taking stands on the issues that were separating his sisters and brothers. Foster contends that only with such an attitude toward fellow Christians can our current crisis be averted, the cycle of division be broken, and the revitalization of the church take place.

The Ones Who Left

It is difficult to illustrate the extreme anti-traditionalist stance in

Churches of Christ. Few statements that reflect deep resentment of our heritage and traditional positions made it into print in the 1990s. Some ultra-traditionalist publications often quoted critical statements by leaders such as Rubel Shelly and Lynn Anderson as examples of the dangers we now face. But these quotes often seem to be taken out of context and interpreted in inflammatory ways. Maybe the reason extreme rejections of our traditional positions were so scarce in the 1990s is that those who were that unhappy with Churches of Christ left or were forced out. Too, some of the angry voices may have become more moderate. And those who have little or no knowledge of why we do what we do don't need to spend time attacking our traditional positions when they feel they can easily set those traditions aside. Whatever the reason, extreme anti-traditional positions cannot be a source of healthy theology for our churches.

There are literally scores of other books and hundreds of articles that attempt to address the crisis in Churches of Christ and suggest remedies for our health and stability, and more are being published every year. We find much to be commended in these writings. In different ways they all show a deep love and concern for our religious heritage. While some are more pessimistic and alarmist than others, they are all confident that Churches of Christ can and must continue to be a vital force in the world for the Kingdom. That is our assurance as well.

Conclusion

This chapter is about identity–an identity that appears to be in jeopardy, an identity that is in crisis. There are two parts to this crisis. The first has to do with whether or not we are the only true Christians. For much of the twentieth century most of us held that assumption, but now it seems to be rapidly eroding. Some fear that if we lose that belief, we lose our very reason for being. Yet we came into existence without any such notion. We wanted to be Christians only, but the claim to be the only Christians never crossed the minds of the founding leaders. Those who insist that abandonment of this exclusive attitude means abandonment of the faith, a repudiation of true Christianity, have themselves abandoned the plea that brought this Movement into existence.

The second part of the crisis has to do with our distinctive beliefs and practices. The attitude that treats our distinctive doctrines and practices as unimportant baggage is as dangerous as any rigid legalistic posture. We believe the teachings that have distinguished Churches of Christ should always be subject to restudy and rethinking in light of God's word. But we are also convinced that those teachings and practices cannot be discarded at will. The positions traditionally held by Churches of Christ have been the subject of more than two centuries of serious and prayerful scrutiny. They have been studied and restudied countless times. Yes, times change. Worship forms and teaching methods that connect in one context may not connect at all in another. Ways of expressing eternal truths that communicate clearly in one age may actually keep people from understanding them in another. Yet casually tossing aside doctrines and practices that have been an integral part of who we are is unhealthy and potentially destructive.

We repudiate an unconcerned and uninformed willingness to drop our distinctive teachings and practices lightly. We equally repudiate stubborn exclusive sectarianism that has decided the right answer to every question before the investigation begins. Neither attitude reflects who we have to be or who we should be.

Here's the point. By getting rid of the notion that we have to be the best or the only Christians to *be* legitimate Christians, we will be free to reexamine ourselves and our teachings seriously without the nagging fear that we might end up losing our identity. Without the burden of believing ourselves to be the only true Christians, we will be able to participate in and contribute substantially to the larger conversation among all followers of Christ and learn some things from it without feelings of betrayal. But it will mean going back to Scripture and thinking deeply about why we do what we do. We must be willing to explain our positions to those both inside and outside Churches of Christ in ways that build up the Kingdom rather than tearing it down. It is to our understandings of Scripture that we now turn.

Chapter 7

Open Bibles and Open Hearts

As the rain and the snow come down from heaven,
and do not return to it without watering the earth
and making it bud and flourish,
so that it yields seed for the sower and bread
for the eater,
so is my Word that goes out from my mouth:
It will not return to me empty,
but will accomplish what I desire
and achieve the purpose for which I sent it.
–Isaiah 55:10–11

When I was growing up, occasionally visitors came to our door witnessing to their church. You know the sort I mean: zealous, narrow, very confident, and brimming over with sectarian tracts designed to convert us to their way of thinking. Their pitch was remarkable. Since we didn't belong to their church, they said that we'd been duped by "the teachings of men" and ensnared by "human traditions." They insisted that what separated our reading of the Bible from theirs is that we *interpreted* the text, while they just let the Bible speak for itself. Their doctrines were those of the Bible, plain and simple. No theology or interpretation involved. So they said.

It bothered me when I realized that these people were playing our tune. This was supposed to be our line, not theirs. We were the ones who denied interpretation, who spoke where the Bible spoke and were silent where the Bible was silent, who taught only what could be established from Scripture, plain and simple. We accused others of having traditions and interpreting the Bible with dogmatic bias, confident that our hermeneutic was open and honest. Yet

> here were people who used the same language, what sounded like the same method, but had come to different conclusions. How could this be? The implications disturbed me. Was I really just reading the Bible for what it says, without interpreting? There must be more to it.
>
> At the time, I knew nothing about the common cultural and intellectual background that made us similar in certain ways to the people standing on our doorstep. We both claimed the Bible as the final authority for Christian faith and practice. We also shared some matching anti-interpretation, anti-tradition arguments that were part of the same nineteenth-century reaction to widespread religious abuses.
>
> –*Jeff*

Reading or Interpreting?

As we saw in Chapter 5, early leaders in the Restoration Movement were asking certain kinds of questions, questions dealing with their needs and circumstances. Questions that fit their world. This affected the way they read Scripture. Like us, they searched the Bible for information that would address their concerns, and address them in ways that made sense in their time and situation.

The truth of God does not change, but God is a living person who seeks a relationship with us humans. Constantly changing human conditions demand a constantly renewed approach to Scripture. This is so partly because we're imperfect and always in need of growth; but growth requires change as we place ourselves under the transformative authority of the Word. Another reason we need a constantly renewed approach to the Bible is that the language of human existence is always on the move. As Campbell demonstrated, the work of translating God's Word into real lives requires fresh work in every generation. A final reason has to do with the

hermeneutic – the set of principles, methods, and rules by which one interprets the Bible

power of the Word itself, since the Word is best communicated through a living witness, as the eunuch discovered on his dusty trip back to Ethiopia. Mere comprehension of ideas doesn't pack the same punch as a living witness whose words and life open up the Scriptures to those needing a Word from God.

After all, today we have our own questions–about appropriate worship styles, the function of the Holy Spirit, fellowship boundaries, modes of evangelism, divorce and remarriage, women's roles, moral purity, social responsibility, the environment, and other things. Some of our questions overlap with those of 200 years ago, many do not. Even where overlap exists, it's not quite the same because the circumstances are different: the culture has changed, a fresh menu of choices is on the table, as it is in every age. We seek God's guidance and the wisdom of Scripture to cope with our questions. It would be a mistake to presume that all the questions have been answered already, partly because some of the questions are new–and partly because authentic answers come only to those who struggle with the text anew to find them.

We must acknowledge that interpretation is inevitable. When young children read, "a little sleep, a little slumber, a little folding of the hands to rest, and poverty will come on you like a robber..." (Proverbs 6:10–11), they figure out pretty quickly that the Bible is not condemning sleep as a sin. A little common sense, a little logic, a little warning from Mom to stay in bed–reason and experience and even relationship play a role in how we read the Bible. Interpretation is a reality. We might all read Proverbs 6 and agree that the Bible is not against sleep but it is not so easy to agree on some other texts. For us and many others, the pursuit of the perfect hermeneutic has been like a grail quest. If we could just hit on the right way to read the Bible, we could guarantee the same results, the right results, every time, as if we were able to reduce the art of interpretation to a scientific formula. An unfortunate side-effect of our quest has been a tendency to deny that we've even been interpreting. This denial can produce self-righteousness and over-confidence about our interpretations. Having to face up to the fact that the grail still eludes us is one of the reasons for the present crisis. Yet one marvelous blessing we've had along the way has been an emphasis on knowing the text of Scripture.

Like the formative leaders of the Restoration Movement, we strongly believe that God speaks to us in a special way in the written Word. We uphold their conviction that the Bible is a divine witness, the revelation of God, inspired by the Father through the Son by means of the Spirit to convict and form his people. It has a unique status and authority, to challenge, question, and correct any other authority brought to the table. This is one of the great emphases of our Movement.

> The Bible is to the intellectual and moral world of man what the sun is to the planets in our system–the fountain and source of light and life, spiritual and eternal.
>
> –Alexander Campbell

It is not enough merely to affirm all this. Biblical literacy is in decline. If we're to move responsibly into the future, one of the most crucial traditions we'll hang on to is that of keeping ourselves under Scripture, but we must do it in a way faithful to Scripture itself. With fresh questions before us, a changing culture around us, and a dawning realization that even our best Bible reading is in fact interpretation and is touched by tradition, we need to be able to plant our feet on something solid. Scripture will play the decisive role.

Reading Less

Why is biblical literacy in decline? Consuming careers, less parental involvement in child-rearing, the influence of entertainment media and the video generation, Bible class trends emphasizing application to the exclusion of content–many factors play a role, perhaps. Another key consideration has to do with the way some traditional modes of reading have sown the seeds of Bible neglect.

By the early-to-mid-twentieth century, it had become common among us to treat the text of Scripture as a collection of facts. Preachers and teachers claimed objectivity–after all, they were just taking the text at face value and striving simply to do what it said, either by direct command, a clear example, or an inference that necessarily followed from something said in the text. They would permit nothing unless it could be punctuated with a clear "thus saith the Lord," a supporting text of Scripture. Or so it seemed.

However, a closer inspection reveals that some strong biases were at work in the way texts were selected, organized and interpreted. Certain topics governed the choice of texts and we had particular favorites. The over-riding question was, "What is necessary for salvation?" We have tended to understand *salvation* as a state of being or an object to possess that gives us the privilege of being admitted to heaven after death. We tended to focus on biblical texts that present salvation this way, highlighting the conditions necessary for being added to the company of the saved.

This emphasis on salvation as an object led us naturally to focus on the external marks of the institution that offers it–the church's organization and governance, how you obtain membership, what could get you kicked out, what the group does when it gets together publicly, its policies, its procedures, its name. Controversial issues of the day about such matters were like magnets, drawing out passages of Scripture pro or con, whether they wanted to come or not. Texts especially adaptable to these purposes became favorites–Acts and Paul, for instance. Texts that were harder to press into service could be sidelined–like the Gospels and the Old Testament. Scripture was like a box of materials to rummage through. By finding all the pieces we could build the once-for-all divine pattern of the institutional church and ensure that those in it would enjoy eternal salvation.

These emphases are not all bad, but they require balance. The method uncovered some important things, but masked or minimized others. Questions about institution, membership, public worship procedures–these are all important identity matters the church should consider regularly. On the other hand, a church is not just institutional identity; it is also mission and purpose. Identity and purpose go together, but if we focus on identity and forget to keep asking about purpose, in time institutional identity becomes purpose. Similarly, at one level salvation is a state and it involves the promise of heaven. However, at another level salvation is a process–we "*are being* saved" (1 Corinthians 1:18). Salvation is dynamic and alive, a present experience of ongoing transformation being worked out within and among us (2 Corinthians 3:18; Philippians 1:6; 2:12–13; 3:12–14; 2 Peter 1:8).

A *patternistic* hermeneutic tends to blind us to these dimensions of the Bible's teaching for the church. As we mean it here, patternism assumes that the Bible is an assortment of specific rules dictating belief and practice in select areas, mainly the institutional topics of church polity, public procedure, and membership requirements. The actions of the New Testament church instruct us in important ways and the desire to attend to those precedents in Scripture is a good one, but patternistic reading is inconsistent with the Bible's full aims and form.

For one thing, when we treat Scripture like a jumbled box of materials, each piece useful but none more important than any of the others, we blind ourselves to the fact that Scripture has a center of gravity and that individual passages have a literary context. Not much of Scripture fits the category of "rules." Nor does the Bible itself suggest that a search for the external forms of the institutional church should be our main filter for reading and applying the text.

Another problem is that the Bible does not give patternistic instructions for much of what we're obliged to do. It's just not possible to cite a direct and detailed scriptural command for everything the church or the Christian needs to do, such as when to meet for worship, what songs to sing, or how to decide on a career. As we saw in Chapter 5, the "silence of Scripture" causes problems for a hermeneutic that presumes the Bible ought to speak directly to every subject of concern to the church. Is Scripture's silence on a topic permissive or prohibitive? Either stance assumes a patternistic approach to Scripture as a rulebook, one that either wants Scripture to provide a direct rule where none is given, or presumes that there may be areas of life on which Scripture lays no claim–a presumption that is also untrue. The Bible speaks a Word into every situation, but it is not by making it into a rulebook that we best hear its voice.

How does all this relate to a supposed decline in biblical literacy? We are experiencing a response to patternism. If the Bible is essentially an assortment of facts to be learned, useful mainly to build and defend a handful of doctrinal patterns about the institutional church, then a person only needs to know so much. Furthermore, the information is good only for a few things. Once you have the facts down and know what to do with them, there's not much left to do. Patternistic reading of Scripture can make us lazy, since it presumes that little or no interpretation is necessary. The aim is to comprehend and accept the facts. Patternism can also make us tired. Some people have given up on Bible reading because they find the cataloguing of data to be stale and lifeless, others because they feel that the cataloguing has already been done. Some of us have experienced a patternism infused with a divisive spirit leading to hostile debate, in-fighting, a narrow inflexible focus, and church splits. Texts meant to proclaim redemption were used to revile, with the collateral damage of killing our motivation to study. This has not been everyone's experience, thankfully, but some have been force-fed the letter of the law so long they now feel a craving for its spirit.

> A recent survey of high school students in Churches of Christ shows that most of our youth do not read their Bibles much. Topping the list of reasons: it's "irrelevant," "boring," "unable to keep my attention," and "simply not helpful."
>
> However, in 1999 and again in 2000, over 500 Abilene Christian University students chose to spend their Spring Breaks, not in Ft. Lauderdale or Corpus Christi, but on mission campaigns to the poor and the lost.
>
> The potential devotion of our youth is unquestionable. But what role the Bible will play is an open question.

Still others show their frustration with patternism in a different way. They haven't given up reading the Bible, but in place of "dead" patternism they've adopted a devotional-pietistic method that gives them the lively personal experience they have yearned for. Instead of letting institutional agendas call the shots, the search for relationship and emotion guides their reading. This kind of reading has become a popular antidote to the old patternism. Pietistic reading has a place, and its intentions are good, but it has its own shortfalls. Like patternism, it typically ignores the literary context of biblical passages, at times doing violence to the intended meaning. It produces private interpretations that may never be subject to the scrutiny of any community beyond its own, which can be arrogant and elitist about its particular style of spirituality. Pietistic reading tends naively to let personal emotional experience be the final judge of genuine Bible interpretation. This perpetuates the trendy myth that the sole aim of Christianity is to help the individual build a good "personal relationship with the Lord." But we must remember that many are vulnerable to this myth precisely because they inherited static methods of reading the Bible that were not at all relational.

We cannot reduce Christianity to ideas or to specific positions on issues. If we read the Bible mostly for the sake of debate and to fortify the institution's boundary markers, we uncover only a small portion of its richness. No wonder many have grown hungry for other aspects of God's revelation, seeking a word from God for the inner person, something to inform the experience of salvation as a dynamic and growing dimension of this present life. They ask: Could there be more to a relationship with God than knowing and keeping his commands about church? Might Scripture provide help for our other relationships too? Does the Bible only list moral rules for us to keep–or does it also provide resources for keeping them? How can we find Bible texts that give a voice to the hungers and joys and aches and doubts of the spirit?

There have always been godly Christian people among us who knew and taught these dimensions of Scripture. Yet in too many places, the Bible was not being used much to nurture the spiritual life. People became hungry and thirsty. The Bible dried up, so they shelved it. Many have turned to other sources for spiritual renewal, feeding on books and tapes and seminars that stimulate them spiritually, perhaps even in place of Scripture. Some of these resources offer rich, solid stuff. But some are as deficient and narrow as the divisive patternism people are running away from. Many popular resources fall far short of reflecting the depth and balance of Scripture, yet because they offer people something they've been missing, they can seem very satisfying, for the moment. The danger is in letting them narrow the priorities of our Bible reading again, according to the special agendas of the new material we're devouring.

These trends of biblical neglect are in full swing, but it's important to realize that they are occurring not because people hate the Bible or have an innate wish to leave us and graze elsewhere. For the most part, it's happening because they hunger for relationship, a living Word, and life in the Spirit.

We need a restoration of respect for biblical authority. However, we cannot properly honor the text's authority unless we're honest about the distance separating us from the text. We are not the original audience of the biblical text, nor is it essentially a book of ordinances immediately portable into our setting. From this standpoint, the problem of "silence" touches all of Scripture, since no verse of it was originally composed directly to address the needs of a twenty-first-century church in America. The distance of language, history, culture, and the fact that we are indirect recipients of literary texts originally aimed at someone else, all create a gap between us and the text. We shouldn't resent the gap, since this is how God has chosen to speak to us through Scripture. Nevertheless it is often into that gap that we pour our biases and preconceptions, using the text in ways that depart from its spirit. Instead, we can bridge the gap in healthy ways if we:

- respect the literary character of the biblical text
- seek to apprehend the theological core of the Bible overall
- cultivate the spiritual disciplines of good reading

The Discipline of Reading with Humility

Though later developments in the Movement have clouded the picture some, its early leaders adopted a good posture towards Scripture, because it was humble and confessional. At the heart of their reading was an invitation to let Scripture challenge them, convict them, reform them. Deliberate submission to the words of the Father imitates Jesus. When we adopt that posture, God does extraordinary things with us through his Word. Yet this takes discipline and watchfulness. We must resist letting our own traditional interpretations become the authority so that we elevate them as idols, convincing ourselves that they are divine and unchangeable just because we can cite chapter and verse. One symptom of this appears when we start aiming the challenging words of Scripture more towards others than towards ourselves. This quality doesn't suit a people called to pick up the cross.

We must be humble enough to admit that we are human. We make mistakes. Even when we aren't making mistakes as such, our situations still affect us and shape the way we read and apply the Bible. We must act as if we really believe that the Word comes by the grace of God, not by human initiative. In other words, the best and most authentic readings of Scripture come to the humble, not the arrogant. God works through human efforts, through human methods and understandings, but he is the one working and what he does goes beyond the capability of any hermeneutic. The gap between us and the text would be too broad for us to close without the activity of God's Spirit, who works in the community to lead us into all truth when we are faithfully cultivating the holy life (John 16:13). Good interpretation is always bathed in prayer.

Our Bible reading should reflect awareness that God is a *Who* rather than a *What*. If we let ourselves be pre-occupied with the *what* or *how* of Christianity, we're surrendering to the temptation to deal only with something we can manage, rather than remaining open to the unmanageable mystery of the person of God. Reading the Bible should lead us to tremble and to wonder, not to set our jaws with audacious certainty. Good reading leads to feelings of love more than a sense of control. It should often lead to silence rather than a loud and smug tone of voice.

We're not advocating an attitude toward Scripture that is uncertain or lacks confidence, one too flimsy for bold proclamation. A weak posture is no good. Neither is a stance of arrogant over-confidence. Somewhere in between arrogance and weakness is healthy *conviction*–the attitude of faith that grounds us firmly on the truth and makes no apologies for its assurance, but is also willing to let truth challenge and reform it. This tone of voice "speaks the truth in love" for the sake of edification (Ephesians 4:15).

We'll be able to maintain this posture of conviction (between arrogance and uncertainty) by placing our weight on the *core* of the biblical witness, not by trying to distribute it over a vast and complicated structure of detailed dogma that threatens to come crashing down with every minute adjustment. Scripture itself is pretty clear about which things matter most. By letting the text speak for itself, we learn that it has its own center of gravity. Getting ourselves oriented on that center comes first.

The Discipline of Reading with Integrity

The search in Scripture for a one-size-fits-all pattern pays attention only to part of the biblical witness–the part that acknowledges the unity of faith. But Scripture also attests to diversity. The assumption that every church should look and act alike does not fit the Bible's testimony. The personality of the church at Corinth in Paul's day does not seem exactly like those of the churches at Philippi or Rome. The attitude of the book of Revelation towards the government differs from that found in Romans 13, and 1 Peter takes a still different angle. The issues of Jewish Christians in the first century were not the same as those of Gentiles. Not that the apostles' teachings were inconsistent or contradictory. They addressed different situations. Yet it's important to notice that, taken as a whole, their instructions are not aimed at making churches uniform. Paul opposed people who pressed for uniformity at any cost, devoting himself instead to preserving a redemptive diversity (1 Corinthians 12; Ephesians 2, 4; Romans 14–15).

During the late Middle Ages, a sort of monolithic society in

Western Europe made religious uniformity a conceivable option for the Roman Catholic church. In that climate, the church largely succeeded in standardizing belief and practice. In our own history, uniformity of faith and practice from one congregation to another–or one generation to another–has only been even theoretically plausible when there was a common cultural ground holding it all together. Since Scripture nowhere presents a complete detailed pattern for the church, patternistic reading leaves many holes. It "works" only when the holes are being filled in the same ways for everyone in the group, usually filled in by culture. The Bible does not tell us what sort of songs to sing, but nobody worried about it much so long as tastes and trends remained the same. As culture has changed and in our churches we encounter people of different history or geographic locale or race or economic background or educational level, we've had to reconsider what diversity means for our churches. It is wrong to be suspicious of differences just because they are differences, or to assume that where one congregation's practice diverges from that of another, one of them must be in error.

On the other hand, it would also be wrong to deny the unity of our faith. Flowing out of the essential unity of the one God is the unity of one body, one Spirit, one hope, one Lord, one faith, one baptism (Ephesians 4:4–6). Yet when Paul recites these hallmarks of the one Christian faith, he does not use them to propel a vision of uniformity. Instead, these items form the platform from which he helps his readers appreciate the *diversity* of the body, as each member receives distinct gifts from Christ and finds distinct roles within the church (Ephesians 4:7–13). *The church exists in a state of unity with diversity.*

Acknowledging unity with diversity involves integrity, because in a patternistic framework, total confidence about each detail is essential and uniformity is expected. Yet God has not promised that we can understand everything. Although the basic teachings of Scripture are plain and simple, in another sense interpretation is not so simple. Parts of the Bible are not easy to understand; even Peter thought Paul's words could be difficult to grasp (2 Peter 3:15-16). More than flawless comprehension, Scripture emphasizes the role of attitude. The person who truly seeks the Lord will find him, as Jesus promised (John 7:17). Only those willing to take a step of faith and invest themselves in his message would be able to understand him (Matthew 13:10-17). It is the spiritual person who understands matters of the Spirit (1 Corinthians 2:12–14).

By contrast, consider the Pharisees whom Jesus criticized. They were experienced and mentally sharp. They had the Word and knew it well. They were masters of the exegetical methods of their day, the same methods used by Jesus and Paul and Matthew. But typically their attitudes were poor and the spirit of their community was sour, so their Bible reading went wrong.

Proper Bible interpretation has more to do with character and attitude than it does with intellectual training and scientific method. Bible study is a kind of worship, an act of devotion. Prerequisites for authentic Bible study and the formation of sound doctrine are piety and holiness. Poets hope that their readers know something about how poetry works. Composers of music insist that we haven't experienced their work unless we hear it performed. Scripture insists that authentic Bible interpretation

> In order to study the Scriptures and understand them correctly, an honorable life, purity of soul, and Christlike virtue are needed.
>
> –*Athanasius of Alexandria*, c.336

happens only when readers accept the claims of the text and live it out (James 1:22-25). Christians involved in service to the poor read Jesus' teachings differently than those who never bother, and their reading of the text is potentially more authentic. Their reading has integrity because it is integrated into their lifestyle.

If we want people to interpret the text of the Bible responsibly, it will not do to train them only intellectually, to tutor them in methods designed to guarantee certain conclusions. Technique and method count, but only to the extent that they grow out of a humble attitude towards the text and further its application. It is true that sincerity of heart does not necessarily produce good interpretation, but it is also true that correct interpretations do not happen where faith or humility are absent. It is possible to do much "in Jesus' name" yet end up on the wrong side (Matthew 7:21–23; 25:31–46). "Getting the facts right" is not the same as "doing the Word," not as James means it.

The Discipline of Reading in Community

Good interpretation is never done in isolation. Reading with integrity compels interpreters to do their work in the context of a faithful community and be responsible to that community. The Bible values the individual, but sees the individual as part of the group. The business of interpretation and discernment requires many people with different gifts and perspectives (1 Corinthians 12-14; Ephesians 4:7-16).

Knowing the full Truth of God (John 14:6) is not just a matter of grasping concepts or nailing down rules. It has to do with relationship–not only with him but also within the body of his Son, the church. The Spirit who guides us into truth works powerfully in the community. The desire to cultivate a vital program of personal Bible reading ought not to eclipse the need for studying with others and for bringing one's own interpretations into conversation with the church's use of Scripture. Interpreters should feel a sense of responsibility and loyalty to the community of faith. Churches should equip their people to read Scripture well, adopting processes of interpretation that give voice to everyone in the community.

Little-known Fact

Of the 2913 times the little word "you" occurs in modern English translations of the New Testament, in 1847 cases the underlying Greek is plural, not singular.

The point? It's easy to miss the fact that the Bible addresses itself mostly to groups. Individuals should apply the text to themselves as part of a group.

This does not mean that our interpretations should ape the existing traditions of the community. Accountability means something else. In practice, it means that the best interpretations will happen where Christians are reading, serving, praying, worshipping together. It means that heritage and tradition count for something. Individual interpreters will study Scripture for the church's sake, seeking the wisdom of the group, subjecting their conclusions to its scrutiny, ensuring that their interpretations address the present needs of their church. For its part, the group will listen carefully to its gifted Bible students, even the lone prophetic voices that arise to rebuke it. The life and ministry of the church will set the questions that really need answering from Scripture, questions about both identity and about mission, questions that will differ somewhat from one congregation to another.

Interpretations connected to the core Gospel that heal relationships and enable the church to work and worship well will be confirmed. Those that damage the core, blocking the church's mission or disrupting its priorities, must be considered flawed, no matter what method produced them or how logical they seem. This is not a surrender to utility, but a desire to let the genuine measures of truth have their say.

Reading from the Center

The only thing that prevents the diversity of Scripture from collapsing into a jumbled mess is the Bible's center of gravity, its core. This core is summarized in the simple confession of the early church, the conviction expressed countless times at baptism: that Jesus is Lord and Messiah, the Son of God. It is the crux of the apostle's message: "in Christ God was reconciling the world to himself, not counting their trespasses against them" (2 Corinthians 5:19). As the eunuch discovered when reading Isaiah, the crucial assumptions necessary for understanding the text have to do with the person and work of Christ (Acts 8:30–35).

The core is our starting point and controls our Bible reading. "If you confess with your lips that Jesus is Lord and believe in your heart that God raised him from the dead, you will be saved" (Romans 10:9). This seems a bit vague. Couldn't the expression, "Jesus is Lord," mean just about anything? Not really. In a patternistic mode of reading, which treats passages like Romans 10:9 as propositional statements about institutional entry requirements, perhaps this would be true. Yet it is possible to read in a way that won't let us get away with such a simplistic interpretation. We can pay attention to the context of the verse. Also, by searching for the center of the biblical message, we can connect the pieces together and align them on the center of gravity–neglecting nothing, but allowing each piece to find its proper place. The few words of this confession are not open to just any understanding. The Bible insists that it means certain things and not others, that it is has particular implications for faith and life. This brief statement, and others like it in Scripture, does not say everything that needs to be said, but it is a good summary principle to govern our reading of Scripture.

We're asserting that the Bible isn't just a repository of facts to be extracted and rearranged into doctrine according to any scheme. We say this because we see in Scripture an overall framework holding all its parts together. Although the Bible has different kinds of literature within it, its overarching framework is one of *story* or *narrative*, not rules. It tells the story of God's saving acts, the human drama that pivots on the events of Christ's life and death and resurrection. The Bible includes facts and data of course, but the facts are embedded in the story and they gain their proper significance based on their role in it. The story comes first.

The Apostles: Witnesses to the Core

Repeatedly in the Old Testament we see that Israel's primary business was to remember the story of God and live like they remembered it (see Exodus 20:1–17). The Apostles follow the same plan. Paul typically gives his readers a sense of the great drama in which they're involved (Ephesians 1–3) before he gives them specific instructions about how to behave (Ephesians 4–6). Description comes before prescription. This is why we've said that the *Who* and *Why* of the story come before the *what* and *how* of biblical religion.

The core story shaped the Apostles' teaching as they extended that story into the life of the church. You can get a feel for the core not by reading piecemeal, but by asking:

What things are mentioned most in Scripture?

What is specifically highlighted as most important?

What things keep showing up at the center of the writers' messages?

The teachings of Scripture spin a web of doctrinal meaning. By tracing the threads to see how they are joined together, we can see what lies in the middle. For example, Paul meditates on the death of Christ in order to resolve internal church conflict (Philippians 2). Peter holds up Christ's example in order to provide resources for Christian living, such as how to get along with non-Christian spouses and employers (1 Peter 2–3). In Revelation, John tries to put the reader in possession of the Lamb's victory, in a world darkened by persecution and the overwhelming pressure to conform culturally. The purpose of the universe is to see everything brought under Christ (Ephesians 1:9–10).

As situations arose and it became necessary to discern the mind of God and provide wise counsel, the Apostles reflected on the person of God and the story of his saving acts, expressed most fully in the death and resurrection of Jesus. This story was their touchstone and their control. The essential elements of the story were non-negotiable and its boundaries

Matters of First Importance

"Now I would remind you, brothers and sisters, of the good news that I proclaimed to you, which you in turn received, in which also you stand, through which also you are being saved, if you hold firmly to the message that I proclaimed to you–unless you have come to believe in vain.

"For I handed on to you as of first importance what I in turn had received: that Christ died for our sins in accordance with the Scriptures, and that he was buried, and that he was raised on the third day in accordance with the Scriptures...."

–1 Corinthians 15:1–4

could not be transgressed (1 Corinthians 15:1–8), nor would just any understanding of the story be allowed. For example, 1 John insists that anyone who denies that Christ came in the flesh, by confession or by ethic, is not truly of God (1 John 4:2–3). Paul contends that those who damage churches in their selfishness can not truly confess Jesus' Lordship (see 1 Corinthians 12:3).

In essence, the core of our faith is the story of our creator God's actions to save us from sin and death, culminating in the life, teaching, death, and resurrection of Christ. It is that God has graciously covenanted with his people in these saving acts, calling people into a relationship with him and incorporating them through baptism into the body of his Son. That body is the church, the dwelling place of God's Spirit, a community called to worship him and to be the expression of Jesus in the world. The body stays connected together and to the Head through its ministry and ritual, such as regular celebration of the Lord's Supper. This is an imperfect summary, but in it are the indispensables–the essential combination of story, event, idea, relationship, individual, community, and ethics, along with the ritual and ceremony that fuse them all together into a blended and spiritual whole.

This summary of the Apostles' teaching shows that their experience with Christ had transformed their lives. They accepted him not only as the authoritative interpreter of Scripture, but its actual interpretation, its fulfillment (Matthew 5:17). As chief interpreter, he gave us some clues about how to do it (Luke 24:45–48). He insisted that certain commands are foundational. The Lord of the Sabbath reminded his disciples that God has priorities:

Witnesses to Core Truth

Around A.D. 165, the Christian scholar Justin was put to death in Rome for his faith. An account of the interrogation shows that persecuted Christians had a firm grip on their central identity:

Rusticus the prefect said, "What kind of doctrine do you profess?"

Justin said, "This: we worship the God of the Christians, whom we consider to be one from the beginning, the maker and designer of all creation, visible and invisible; and the Lord Jesus Christ, the Son of God, who had been preached beforehand by the prophets as about to appear among humankind, the herald of salvation and teacher of good disciples."

It was by witnessing just such an event years earlier that Justin himself had been converted.

About 10 years later in Gaul, a young man named Sanctus braved the torture of red-hot metal plates by repeating incessantly, "I am a Christian. I am a Christian." He became a hero of the faith.

In a climate hostile to faith, early Christians were compelled to be clear on what mattered. In our own age, the pressures of an increasingly secular world challenge us not to let pre-occupation with peripheral matters drain the vitality out of our witness.

Hear, O Israel: The Lord our God, the Lord is one.

You shall love the Lord your God with all your heart,

and with all your soul, and with all your might.

You shall love your neighbor as yourself: I am the Lord.

Deuteronomy 6:3–5;
Leviticus 19:18
(Matthew 22:34–40)

The Father desires "mercy and not sacrifice." Justice and mercy are "weightier matters." External religious observances weigh something too. They count. But they stay in proper balance only when we let the weightier matters be our standard of measurement (Matthew 12:7; 23:23; Hosea 6:6). One antidote to the hazards of patternism is this dependence on the core–not to hammer the Bible flat, but to let the grain of its texture emerge by recognizing its center of gravity and striving to stay aligned with it. To give a cup of cold water in Jesus' name is to act out of that core, to hold the center of gravity (Matthew 10:42; 25:44–45). This action in turn sharpens our eyesight so we can discern the core even more clearly when we come back to the text again, recognizing that in Scripture some things weigh more than others.

A Christian reading of Scripture keeps Jesus' teaching and person central, allowing his interpretation of what it means to love God and love neighbor be in control. He interprets it not only by his teaching, but by his life and example, by his death on the cross and by his resurrection. He himself is the meaning of it all. The Apostles help us see how this works in practice. For Paul, Jesus' life, death, and resurrection are core values that have implications for how we relate to God, how we treat people, and for moral purity. He refers to these values constantly. They also connect to certain external observances that are integral to our participation in the story and formative of the ethics near the core–baptism and the Lord's Supper chief among them. The farther something is from the core, the less central its role. Paul was more flexible with circumcision and food laws, for example. In fact, he wouldn't tolerate any demand to observe those practices when the demand violated the substance of the core Gospel (see Galatians 1–2).

Staying on Center

We want to be faithful to the intent of Scripture. We want to be able to append a "thus saith the Lord" to all of our teachings and practices, but this is not a simple matter of citing texts as direct commands. Jesus and the Apostles show us the plan for good Bible interpretation: read Scripture from within its own narrative framework, catch a glimpse of what God has done in Christ, and seek to emulate that, keeping a sense of the big picture. Our obedience to rules is not at the core. God's gracious saving acts are. True, rules are a part of faith, and rules form a part of the text that we interpret. Churches should not be afraid to teach the Christian rules of faith and practice and behavior, but rules take their proper place only in relation to the core. Furthermore, it's only by living at the core that we gain the resources we need to keep the rules.

Otherwise, strange things illegitimately crowd out the weightier matters, becoming our standard of faith. What we adopt as the core has a way of perpetuating itself, of ensuring its own survival. It wants to organize everything to its liking. It can deceive us. For instance, it can hoodwink us into thinking that the reason for observing the Lord's Supper every week is because it is commanded as a rule, when the real reason to do it is because it celebrates the core event of God's salvation. The difference between the two reasons is huge–and the contrast between the two styles of spirituality each one feeds is astounding.

We are reading from the center when our governing questions have to do with Scripture's overall plot and its implications for applying the text today. The answers to the questions ought to reaffirm the core Gospel, with our central response of loving God and neighbor in imitation of Jesus as an attempt to flesh out that core. Otherwise they have missed something. In this way, the core of Scripture is a control on our reading, a test to see if we're being faithful to God's essential purposes.

For example, any teaching that neglects the fact that in salvation God graciously takes the initiative and we are the recipients is a teaching that contradicts the dynamic of grace. God's grace is an essential component of the story. Habitual neglect of the doctrine of grace produces distorted versions of the story. This distortion has exposed itself before, as whenever preachers cannot bring themselves to talk about Paul's discussion of the saving effects of confession and belief (Romans 10:9) without adding, "but of course baptism is necessary, etc." We can't just let Paul say what he wants to say. Eventually, people will realize that this off-center partiality does not fit the core of Scripture. A renewal of emphasis on grace will occur. We've seen this very thing happening among us.

Unfortunately, patterns of correction tend to produce over-reactions. The new emphasis on grace, so long neglected, assumes the place of the core, and the story gets over-written as if it were *only* about this one feature of God's grace. Leaning hard the other way, people find they can't bring themselves to use language of duty and responsibility any more, and they may have a hard time talking about the importance of behavior and of external observances. We're human after all; it's hard for us to keep all the priorities in balance they way God does. Much of the history of heresy can be understood as the story of what happens when someone emphasizes one truth of the Christian faith to the exclusion of other crucial truths of the faith.

The tendency to swing with the pendulum is why it's important never to presume that our *understanding* of the core is the same as the core itself. Remember that at the core of the story is a tale of Jesus' submission and humility, a sacrifice of will for the sake of doing the Father's will. With open hearts, we invite our reading of the text to challenge even our understanding of the core so that our thinking is not self-serving. The Gospels remind us that disciples of Jesus tend not to understand things as clearly as they think they do.

A proper attitude towards God and his revelation invites correction and growth.

Reading the Bible as Literature

We thank God that there has never been a famine of his Word among us. In spite of occasional weaknesses and darker moments, we have had good preaching and teaching and a persistent belief in the sufficiency of Scripture. God has graciously raised up people among us who read Scripture through the eyes of faith from a humble posture and who instinctively perceived that the Bible has a center of gravity, that some things are weightier than others. There's the elderly sister who read her Bible through many times but was always ready to learn something new and grow a little. There's the brother who maintained a life of prayer and service in the Kingdom, putting his Bible reading to work by promoting peace in the church. God has worked through people like this to keep his Word alive and his church faithful.

God also has blessed us with biblical scholars, past and present. Many grew up in churches devastated by conflicts arising when Bible reading was enslaved to dogmatic bias and made to serve sectarianism. Their historical and literary training enabled them to blow the whistle on unquestioned biases and put the text back on top. They have taught us to be critical of ourselves in helpful ways.

They have also taught us to revere the text's authority by honoring *the literary nature of the text*. No hermeneutic is sacred. But methods of reading that force us to wrestle with literary context and genre have been like loyal bloodhounds, catching many of our prejudices. Instead of ripping passages out of context and citing them in support of predetermined conclusions, we should do our best to use techniques that preserve the Bible's internal literary authority. If the results challenge cherished traditional conclusions, so be it. Letting the Bible challenge us repeatedly is in keeping with the best instincts of our heritage.

Books of the Bible *develop arguments or have themes*. We should understand passages in the context of the developing ideas and messages of specific books, not as self-standing statements or isolated propositions. Since no verse in the Bible was written directly to us, we should take care not to apply texts in ways that contradict the original purpose for which they were written. Modern editions of the Bible may be segmented into chapters and verses for handy reference, but good Bible reading will pay attention to context.

We must also respect *genre*. The Bible is literature, and contains a number of different genres, different literary forms. Each literary form plays by its own rules, functioning best when we allow it to do for us what it means to do. We don't read fairy tales by the same rules we use to read a news story. They are written according to particular conventions and they are to be read according to those conventions. Some genres major in ideas, others in feelings, others in story. Wisdom and Gospel and Epistle all function differently and we ought to interpret them differently because each conveys information in its own way. Each intends to have a particular kind of effect on the reader. It would be a serious mistake to read Proverbs 22:6, "train children in the right way, and when old, they will not stray," as if it were a divine promise. Wisdom literature is not meant to convey promises but to present us with general truths gleaned by observation. That's the way the genre of Wisdom works. Being honest with the literary character of the Bible is not the only concern here. The nature of God is at stake. Patternistic reading tends to try forcing God into a small box, whereas the diverse material of Scripture shows us how deep and multi-faceted he is.

Of course, even these responsible methods of reading the Bible have their limitations. One real danger is to obsess over the re-creation of a literary moment in history (exegesis), without perceiving the larger story to which it belongs (theology) and laying our story alongside it in order that we may be instructed and transformed as we are integrated into the old story (hermeneutics). In other words, the danger is of being stuck in history without a way to bring the text forward to speak to the needs of today's church. Also, critical exegetes may be tempted to place too much confidence in their methods and their judgment, defending their interpretations as beyond question. On the other hand, some literary approaches sideline concerns for original intent and history so effectively that they easily become the cunning operatives of narrow agendas. Since complete objectivity is impossible, they say, why try?

Some of the Most Common Genres in the Bible

Narrative
Law
Prophecy
Poetry
Epistle
Apocalyptic
Parable
Wisdom

Despite these problems, it would be disastrous to give up on approaches to Scripture that read it as literature and that pay attention to historical context. Pure objectivity may be a myth, but one effective way to check our understanding of the core against the witness of Scripture is to do our best to let the texts speak on their own terms. The tools of history, language, and literary analysis open our eyes to the text's strangeness, so we can get outside ourselves. It's true that we begin the process of Bible reading in faith, with a presupposed core in mind, but our process of interpretation should include moments when we do our absolute best to suspend those presuppositions and let the text challenge us. When practiced with a humble and prayerful heart in the service of the Kingdom and in faithful adherence to the biblical core, the rigorous discipline of literary methods helps us liberate the text from sheer dogmatism.

Reading the Whole Bible

Honesty in the face of the text depends not only on taking the text seriously, but on taking it all. One enemy of healthy diversity in the church is a reading program that neglects the broad diversity of Scripture. The only Bible the New Testament churches had was the Old Testament, after all, and it's heartening to see people giving more attention to it these days. This trend must continue. Patternism is typically narrow in its choice of texts. By contrast, when we read Scripture for a deeper "pattern," a pattern at the level of principles and of core, we are easily able to agree with Paul that Leviticus speaks to us as authoritatively as anything else in the Bible. New Testament authors assumed that Christians were intimately familiar with the Old Testament, or would come to be so. Any attempt to restore the New Testament church must restore its Bible: the Old Testament.

> Patternism tends to discard large chunks of Scripture as mostly irrelevant, shelving anything that won't fit into the predetermined grid or fulfill the aim of directly building an institutional pattern.

The Old Testament is not just background material or an anthology of stories which, when suitably edited, become appropriate fodder for children's classes. It's true that the New Testament claims

Jesus Christ is the most full revelation of God's character and nature. Yet much of what this means is actually fleshed out in the Old Testament where we learn so much about the person of God and how he desires to relate to us. We don't pretend that the business of relating the Old Testament to the New Testament is easy. But the solution is not to discard the Old Testament. Instead, we can follow Paul's lead (he took it from Jesus), reading the Old Testament through a Christ-centered lens. For Paul, the picture took shape around the basic tenets of the faith, with emphasis on the "weightier matters." When we don Christ-centered reading lenses, we discover that the weightier matters of one Testament tend to be those of the other. We may find that Leviticus has important things to say to our worship and our lifestyles today–but perhaps not in the sense of prescribing strict legal patterns. The texture of the Old Testament is profoundly rich, spoken into many different life situations. We're only beginning to appreciate the deep spiritual resources available to us there.

Our reading of the New Testament needs to be comprehensive also. We should beware of camping out on favorite texts or of reading other texts only to see how we can relate them to our favorites. Doing so threatens to perpetuate prejudice and dishonest thinking, undercutting our ability to confirm that our center of gravity is the same as that of Scripture. It's all right to have favorite texts, so long as we realize that Scripture has some favorites too, and that its favorites should be in charge.

Conclusion: Reading with an Attitude

Some of the directions our Bible reading has taken over the

years have not been in keeping with the best instincts of our Movement. This chapter has been more concerned with attitude toward Scripture than a presentation of exegetical and hermeneutical method. We can build on the foundational strengths of Bible reading in our churches by modeling and teaching attitudes to Scripture that recognize the prerequisites of good interpretation:

- Good interpretation begins with the cultivation of virtue by reading with humility, with integrity, and in community.
- Good interpretation acknowledges the Bible's own claims to have a core, or center of gravity, allowing that core to govern both the reading of the text and its application.
- Good interpretation places itself under the text by honoring the text's literary character, respecting genre, context, themes, and textual diversity.

To the question, "Is the silence of Scripture prohibitive or permissive?" we answer: that question is the wrong question, because it assumes the Bible functions mainly as a rulebook. Broadly speaking, we uncover the wisdom of Scripture for a situation not by clamping a stranglehold on a proof-text at the surface level and forcing it to become a direct rule. Nor can we be satisfied merely to check Scripture to ensure that no passage directly forbids something we're proposing to do. Instead, we uncover Scripture's wisdom by prayerfully trying to find relevant biblical principles and apply them to the situation in ways that flesh out the Bible's core.

This does not happen in a vacuum. Right interpretation does not happen outside of contexts where it is being applied faithfully. Good Bible reading comes fully alive only when grounded in the vital stability of heritage and connected to the fresh challenges of a church's unfolding story. Factors of past and present will affect how the Bible shapes a church's response to its situation. In the next chapter, we will further develop some of the topics introduced in this chapter in an exploration of the conditions necessary for healthy doctrinal formulation.

Chapter 8

Sound Doctrine, Healthy Church

Do not infect that heavenly philosophy of
Christ with human decrees.
Let Christ remain what he is, namely the
center, while various circles surround him.
Do not remove the target from its position.
–Desiderius Erasmus of Rotterdam (1518)

It is a time of momentous change in the church. The older, reliable leaders are fading from the scene, leaving inexperienced and sometimes wayward youngsters in charge. The distance between the generations is increasing, with little mutual respect shared between old and young. The social pressures are enormous, causing many to compromise their values for the sake of fitting into the culture. People are not reading their Bibles as they should, and when they do they're apt to come up with bizarre interpretations. The church is at a loss to know whom to look to for leadership–what it means to be a good leader seems to be up for grabs in some places. Worldly standards of success are competing with divine standards, and cliques are forming around the personalities of persuasive leaders. Petty bickering and trivial issues threaten to obscure the core values of the church, disrupting its mission and ripping it apart from the inside out. Crucial doctrines seem about to be forgotten. If something isn't done pretty fast, there will be nothing left of the church in the next generation–or what is left will have been so disfigured that it will be unrecognizable as the church.

Sounds familiar. But we're talking about the first-century church of Paul's day, the churches Paul has in mind when he writes the Pastoral Epistles (1-2 Timothy, Titus). The Apostles will not be on hand forever. Paul's task is to train and equip discerning church leaders who will guide the church into the future. As the Gentile church expands, moving into new environments constantly, leaders need to face the challenges flexibly. Yet they must also remain faithful, adapting in ways that preserve the integrity of the core without compromise, building on the wisdom of existing foundations. Paul gives some practical instructions, yet he tailors them to the specific situations at Ephesus and Crete, a detail that surfaces when we notice that the instructions in one book differ somewhat from those in another (e.g., compare 1 Timothy 3:1–13 with Titus 1:5–9). Facing the future is not a simple matter of getting all the institutional forms and rules and procedures right, nor will each church look just like the other. For Paul in the Pastoral Epistles, it is a matter of getting the attitudes right, of creating and sustaining a healthy environment of doctrinal reflection. "Sound doctrine" does not mean accurate doctrine, correct doctrine. It means healthy doctrine. Healthy doctrine is correct doctrine, of course, but the difference in emphasis is important. Soundness is equivalent to health, something the yardstick of "correctness" is not particularly well suited to measure.

A Biblical Model

The Pastoral letters highlight the necessary ingredients of healthy doctrinal formation. First of all, the foundation of everything

Paul does is his *faith*, born out of an experience of God's calling and grace (1 Timothy 1:1, 12–14; 2 Timothy 1:8–12; Titus 1:1–3). Paul knows that God has made the first move, that the work is his, that prayer should be the most prominent phenomenon in any ministry (1 Timothy 2:8; 4:5). Paul relies on his faith for guidance in hard times. He expects Timothy and Titus to do the same, reflecting on their own initial experiences of faith and calling, humbly making choices consistent with those experiences (1 Timothy 1:18; 6:12–14; 2 Timothy 3:14; Titus 1:5). This faith is personal, but not private. Relationships with others pervade its origins–in Timothy's case, Paul alludes to "many witnesses." Furthermore, Paul's instructions throughout show that the needs of the community are interwoven with the growth and expression of their personal faith.

Second, *core doctrine* must be preserved. Some things are worth taking a bullet for in "the good fight of the faith" (1 Timothy 1:18; 6:12), but we need to be discriminating. Guard against allowing peripheral matters, such as "myths and endless genealogies," to assume center stage (1 Timothy 1:3–4; 4:3–7; Titus 1:13–14; 3:9–11), no matter how loudly (or deviously) some misguided persons protest that their pet interests are of prime importance (1 Timothy 6:3–5; 2 Timothy 2:16–18; 3:6–7; 4:3–4; Titus 1:10–11). The real villains are not those who eat certain foods, but those who insist that it really matters whether or not you eat certain foods. Those who blaspheme Christ by damaging his church in the name of their own cause are especially corrupt.

Healthy doctrine begins with the belief that God, wanting all people to be saved, has mediated redemption through Jesus Christ. The crux of Christian belief can be summarized briefly in easily repeatable statements (1 Timothy 2:3–6; 3:16; 2 Timothy 2:8,

11–13). Topics not in close orbit around the core are less important, with less at stake. For example, when tested against the content and ethics of the core Gospel, the doctrinal concerns of the troublemakers in Ephesus fail sadly. That is why Paul censures them.

The Pastorals mention grace often. The doctrine that salvation is a work of grace is central and not to be compromised, but a true grasp on grace purifies behavior (Titus 2:11–12) and high ethical standards always accompany true faith. "We know that the law is good, if one uses it legitimately," Paul says (1 Timothy 1:8). Christian faith is more than ideas or propositions: "if we have died with him, we will also live with him." (2 Timothy 2:11) Doctrine and life go together (1 Timothy 4:16). Correctly centered, healthy doctrine has the goal of "love, that comes from a pure heart, a good conscience, and sincere faith" (1 Timothy 1:5). Right behavior will prove right doctrinal orientation that conforms "to the glorious gospel of the blessed God" (1 Timothy 1:10–11; 2 Timothy 2:19). This is why church leaders are to be distinguished mainly by their moral character and servant qualities (1 Timothy 3:1–13; 5:1–20; Titus 1:5–16; 2:2–4). Right behavior is an expression of the grace one has received.

The third observation grows out of the last one, that *ministry* is a fundamental component of Christian doctrine. Paul summons Timothy and Titus to sacrificial service and commands that deacons, elders, widows, and others be trained for ministry. The steadfast church is one in which people offer themselves as God's utensils of service, to be poured out as drink offerings (2 Timothy 2:20–21; 4:6). They pray, they share their wealth generously (1 Timothy 2:1; 6:18), and generally devote themselves to doing good (Titus 3:8, 14). When the church is pursuing its mission with passion, its activity creates a living framework from within which it can teach the truth and make faithful decisions. A biblical view of doctrine as multi-faceted reminds us that sound doctrine does not exist where redemptive ministry is not happening. Ministry is not only the result of sound doctrine but also a pre-requisite.

Fourth, healthy church doctrine is dependent on the dynamic links within a close-knit *community*. The church is God's household and claims its members as family (1 Timothy 3:15). In this family, people nurture and form one another across the generations (Titus 2:3–5), serving one another in prayer and hospitality (1 Timothy 5:5, 10). Christians associate frequently, though they must be sure that their intimate connections with one another are pure and edifying, not injurious to the church (2 Timothy 2:16–17; 3:6; Titus 1:11). They should feel responsible for one another, so much so that those who stray from the center are to be warned or rebuked. Setting an example is part of the Christian life (1 Timothy 4:12). Many of Paul's instructions presume the need for a close familiarity with one another's lives and households.

Fifth, the core faith is preserved and perpetuated through a process of passing on *tradition*. Paul received this tradition and it was handed on to Timothy and Titus, who are themselves obligated to pass it on (1 Timothy 1:11; 2 Timothy 1:13–14; 2:2; Titus 1:9). This tradition seems to have as its foundation the body of teaching that communicates the essence of the Gospel story as Paul has been proclaiming it in his preaching ministry, encapsulated in several memorable brief statements. As his letters show, Paul is skilled at adapting this core message to the needs of different circumstances. Here he appeals to the tradition as an important resource for church leaders facing critical decisions, a unifying and stabilizing force.

The first means of passing on the tradition is the act of teaching, mainly on the part of Timothy and Titus, it seems, but in various contexts other men and women are to join them in the work of conveying the faith. Also, though the conventional teaching methods of the day no doubt played a large part, it's obvious that the church's acts of worship, ministry, and fellowship were also vehicles for transmitting the faith in its fullness. These facets of church life fit together so that the Christian is not merely educated in doctrinal facts but is spiritually formed.

Finally, the text of *Scripture* (here the Old Testament) plays a uniquely authoritative role, one before which all parties must be open and humble. Even Paul answers to the text. It is an external and permanent standard, inspired by God for teaching, training, correcting, and rebuking (2 Timothy 3:16–17). Scripture stands apart from the tradition, in a sense. Yet it is "through faith in Christ Jesus" that they are to read the text (2 Timothy 3:15). Like us, Paul and his pupils are dealing with a text not written directly to them. The Gospel core provides the lens by which they are to understand Scripture, the rule of priority by which they rank the Bible's teachings, the model governing their application. Leaders ought to learn the Scriptures well, proclaiming the Word constantly in ways that illuminate the essential Gospel message and are illuminated by it (1 Timothy 4:13).

Ingredients of Healthy Doctrinal Reflection

Faith
Core Doctrine
Ministry & Piety
Community
Tradition
Scripture

Scripture, faith, core doctrine, tradition, community, ministry, and piety. All inter-related. All integral. And, we hope, all recognized by the reader as important emphases throughout our book. When properly correlated, they form together the ingredients of a church well suited to face crisis moments in ways that defend the faith and honor God. Doctrine is not healthy doctrine unless in its formation and practice it reflects a proper synthesis of the same factors that Paul nurtured in the churches at Ephesus and Crete through Timothy and Titus.

Formulating Doctrine in Churches of Christ

Like Paul, we find ourselves formulating doctrine mainly in response to situations. Our churches will not look quite like the ones he knew, because the setting is different, but the core should remain intact. Paul gave specific instructions because he had specific churches in mind. Underlying those instructions are the more general principles we can apply today. The rest of this chapter draws on our survey of the Pastorals and expands on the observations of Chapter 7 in an attempt to stimulate thinking about healthy doctrinal reflection in our churches.

The Aim: Salvation. In the Pastoral letters, salvation is at stake, but not just salvation in the sense of a ticket to heaven, though that is in view. It is also salvation as a life process of becoming an ever more useful implement in God's hands. It is knowledge, but knowledge that changes us, producing godliness in this life (1 Timothy 4:8; Titus 1:1; 2:11–14). This salvation rests on the hope of eternal life, but taking hold of that life transforms us now (Titus 1:2; 1 Timothy 6:12). In Scripture, salvation is not only a state that can be gained or summarily lost. Such a purely static view of salvation can lead us to focus all our energies on ensuring accuracy in certain areas so that we don't lose our status as "saved." Or it can lead us to fixate on the goal of bringing people into the church, of increasing membership, so they too can enjoy the state of having been saved. But alongside the worthy goals of guarding the borders of the Kingdom and of enlarging them numerically, the church has the task of expanding God's reign in the hearts of people and within the life of the community of faith–the task of nurturing spiritual growth.

Salvation is not just a state, it is also a process of growth and transformation. It is a living thing that depends on the inter-relationship of many factors, such as Scripture, individual faith, connection to church community, tradition, and active love. For this reason, we find it difficult to know how best to list the conditions of healthy doctrinal reflection. The following sequence does not do them justice, since each item touches all the others–when something happens in one area, it affects all the rest.

An Attitude of Faith. First, a word about risk and trust. We need to resign ourselves humbly to the fact that there is no way to remove all risk from the decision-making process. The experiment to find an absolutely fool-proof method guaranteeing unquestioned results did not succeed. We are not as smart as we had hoped. Nor can we abdicate responsibility by claiming that the Bible addresses our issues so directly that no interpretation will be required. We're obliged to develop the discipline of responsible interpretation, but control and certainty are not within our power.

Formulating doctrine involves trusting God. When we acknowledge that God is the initiator of our religion, it's easier to put matters into his hands. Sometimes we act as if our job is to control everything that happens and to pass judgment on every result. It is true that God did not create us to be spectators. He honors us by inviting us to partner with him in his work, hoping that we will mature under his care and instruction. We have responsibilities as his children. Nevertheless, we must trust in the Lord's promise that the Spirit will guide us into truth (John 16:13).

We want to please God, but our main job is not to get everything right. Our job is to live by the right story. It was the open and confessional attitude, the posture of faith, that set the centurion of Capernaum above his learned Jewish neighbors. Truly seeking to love God and love neighbor is the best way to minimize risk. Rather than trusting falsely in a particular hermeneutical method, a better strategy for relieving doubt might be the development of the spiritual disciplines of prayer, fasting, and meditation, since by them we learn how to rely on God. This would be a healthy complement to the intellectual discipline of responsible literary interpretation.

Expect to be surprised from time to time. Sometimes the result of a process of doctrinal reflection will be a change that you didn't anticipate or even want. On the other hand, there will be times when a healthy process of doctrinal reflection affirms the status quo, just when you were looking for a change.

The Bible. Wise doctrinal decisions are based on Scripture. We need to continue developing the discipline of Bible study. We need to examine our preaching and teaching and our family lifestyles to see whether Scripture is playing the role it ought to at home and in church. Scripture should set the standard of faith and practice, providing Christians and churches with the story by which they live. We advocate a conservative approach to Scripture–one that honors the text as literature. Our reading should be honest with the text, reflecting the attitudes we discussed in Chapter 7 and using methods of Bible reading that keep us under its authority. We should resist the temptation to be liberal with the literary character of the

What is Theological Liberalism?

MISUSE OF TERMS	CORRECT USE OF TERMS
Conservative–someone who adheres to the practices and teachings typical of Churches of Christ in the 1950s	Conservative–someone who respects the Bible's authority, letting it speak on its own terms (and even to correct traditional beliefs and practices)
Liberal–a change agent who advocates or allows alteration in traditional practices or teachings	Liberal–someone who denies the authority or accuracy of Scripture, emphasizing the ability of human reason to discover truth on its own

Some have been using these terms as defined on the left, but the right-hand column explains what a true biblical conservative is. It is possible to be biblically conservative while being institutionally liberal, because an honest respect for the text of Scripture will regularly lead us to reform the institution of the church as it exists in the world. We shouldn't jump to the conclusion that someone who advocates change in the church is liberal—not theologically liberal, at least.

text (and its inherent core) for the sake of conserving institutional norms. A conservative approach to Scripture may require a "liberal" approach to the institution, a willingness to change what we've been doing as an institution, but this is not biblical or theological liberalism. The teaching of Scripture has contours. We should find them. This in itself will renew the text for many people.

The Core. Healthy doctrinal formulation cannot get far if we assume that every doctrine or practice is as important as every other one. All of Scripture is important, but as we saw in the last chapter, the Bible itself makes it clear that the importance of every teaching is relative to the center. In some doctrines and practices, much is at stake–anyone who minimizes the grace of God is accursed

(Galatians 1:8), those who deny the saving flesh and blood of Jesus are Antichrist (1 John 2:22; 4:3), the church that makes the Lord's Supper a travesty of loving communion is held accountable for injuring the body of the Lord (1 Corinthians 11:27). But sometimes we've acted as if everything is at stake in practically every question. It's true that even peripheral matters have significance, but they should not be allowed to eclipse the crux, throwing everything off balance. There will always be some disagreement about just what the non-negotiables are, but the discussion will have a better chance of going where it needs to go if we at least accept the biblical principle that a core exists.

This doesn't mean that when articles of belief and practice are more distant from the core, they don't matter. This mistake is easy to make. It may be true that much of what we do and how we do it can flex to meet new needs, but everything is still accountable to the core, it should all flesh out the core. For some of us, focusing on Scripture's core is the challenge to remove some pet doctrines out of the center that don't belong there. For others, it's the challenge to recognize that more belongs at or near the core than they've allowed. In the words of the Christian pop artist Clay Crosse, "It all comes down to a man, dyin' on the cross, savin' the world." He's right. But more needs to be said. Christianity is not just a sincere feeling about Jesus. As much as God's heart breaks over denominational division, as much as we take exception to attitudes that elevate peripheral doctrines to salvation status, correct doctrine still counts in Christianity.

There are right ideas. And wrong ones. There are real historical events at the core. There are essential practices which link idea and event–baptism and the Lord's Supper. Also, wrong ideas eventually end up taking you to the wrong places. Liberal groups who years ago decided to ditch chunks of the doctrinal content of the Christian faith in order to pursue the admirable goal of social justice now find themselves bankrupt of any basis for their social agenda because they cut out the heart. Without the core Gospel, it's impossible to sustain the Christian mission and a Christian set of values.

Furthermore, without the *whole* core, we become lop-sided slaves of the latest trends and overreactions. In the New Testament, we see that the core Gospel is about grace–but it's also about responsibility. The Gospel compels us to evangelize, finding ways to connect with people in the world–but it also calls us to reflect God's holiness in the distinct "otherness" and strangeness of our community. Staying centered corrects imbalances. The danger of recognizing the core is not that it makes some things trivial. Instead, it insists that we admit the importance of *everything* we do, but in a way that keeps the center central.

Community Discernment. The individualism of our age has led us to imagine that the Christian walk could be a solo endeavor, just "me and Jesus." This tendency in our churches is partly a reaction to the institutional focus of our heritage, but it is mostly a surrender to the deep currents of individualism running through the fabric of our modern society. In a past generation, we heard, "My faith and salvation are between me and God." Today, we hear, "The only thing that counts is my personal relationship with God." These are two sides of the same coin. Scripture never envisions such a thing. The quest for a "personal relationship with the Lord" has rich potential, but sometimes it deflects what God is trying to do through relationships in the church. It's important to notice that when Paul says, "continue to work out *your* salvation with fear and trembling"

(Philippians 2:12), the Greek pronouns and verbs are plural. The "working out" is the activity and mutual inter-dependence of a group, not the effort of an individual; the "salvation" in view here is a corporate experience.

Today we are seeing much attention focused on the personal indwelling of the Holy Spirit in individual Christians. Not a bad topic. It's biblical. But Scripture focuses more on *the role of the Spirit in the community*. The Gospel of John, the book of Acts, many places in Paul's letters, all stress the role of the Spirit in the church, as guide and equipper and source of power for the community of believers, not primarily for individuals. So much of the current interest in giftedness stresses the individual, perhaps owing more to the secular values of being personally fulfilled and of finding work you enjoy. For some, the community exists only to provide a platform for individuals to exercise their gifts and express their unique talents. But in passages like 1 Corinthians 14, Ephesians 4:4–16, and 1 Peter 4:7–11, the emphasis is on the fact that individual gifts are given for the church. The emphasis is not on the individual. Personal fulfillment or enjoyment are not factors. Keeping the correct balance and emphasis in this area is as hard today as it was in the first century.

Historically, a high regard for church has been one of the strengths of our Movement. The church exists as God's instrument for restoring relationships between himself and his people, and among the people themselves (Ephesians 2). The Bible calls this *salvation*, and it's available only through Christ and his church. It requires something our culture is reluctant to allow: a high sense of accountability to the community. It requires something, which we, under the influence of culture, have often been reluctant to allow:

accountability to the church in our Christian walk and in our reading of Scripture.

We need an approach to doctrine that respects both sides–the work of God in the individual and the work of God in the community. The unity and diversity inherent in the body of Christ expresses itself well when a church involves its people in the process of doctrinal formulation. In the spirit of Acts 15, a church sometimes needs to gather its people to consider what God is doing among them and how, in the light of Scripture, they can respond most faithfully. Discussion groups, public teaching, elders' consultations of members–churches must find various ways to give individuals a voice and to bring the whole group in on a conversation, allowing its collective wisdom to speak. At a time when church educational programs and other ministries too often find themselves in complicity with the secular forces that sub-divide people by age and interest group for the sake of convenience or to cater to market groups, we need to do the hard work of putting people back together into the extended church family in an effort to heal some of the fragmentation ailing our society.

Diversity of every sort is widening in many of our churches. Diversity complicates things, but generally we ought to welcome it, since a diverse congregation is liable to be healthier than one whose homogeneity suggests an imbalanced and narrow agenda. Diversity opens up for us the richness of our Lord. It is the diverse church that best expresses Jesus' presence in the world–no one disciple can do or be all that Christ is. He was able to reach wealthy tax collectors, Gentiles in the military, peasant women, and Jewish religious leaders. Jesus' disciples will find different areas in which to serve and flourish, opening up different aspects of Jesus' character. Some appreciate best his open love, mercy, and compassion; others remind us of his high standards for discipleship and purity. Some remind us of the virtues of simple, trusting faith from the heart; others show us the importance of serious study and the need to search out the Father with our intellects. Respectful conversation within community can form our perspectives in surprising ways.

Having them all present, giving them all a voice guards us against the common abuse of privileging one agenda, or even of elevating one style of spirituality over others that are equally valid. This isn't about striking a happy medium, but about letting the church flesh out Christ's body in its fullness. The church needs to be a place comfortable with Paul, who travels and preaches; with Anna, devoted to prayer; with Priscilla and Aquila, who teach in their home; with James, who has a knack for cutting through issues and finding peaceful solutions; with Lois, gifted at shaping a child's faith; with Dionysius the Areopagite, a learned philosopher; with Barnabas, who encourages by word and financial contribution; and with fishermen, who bring only their willing hands, strong backs, a simple faith, and a deep love for Jesus.

We become more like Christ corporately as each gifted part connects to and interacts with the other, working together (Ephesians 4:7–16). The task of leadership in Ephesians 4 is to equip the church for service by bringing each part together, so that we sharpen each other, call gifts out of one another, and open doors for each other. This is where active ministry and relationships make the needs and problems and joys very real. This is where various points of view converge, challenge, and enrich each other. This is where disciples discover how to use their natural abilities to glorify God and bless the church–and also where they learn the discipline of doing the things that don't come so naturally but need to be done anyway. Only then do we "grow up into him." Only then are we "no longer infants," but become stable and mature enough to sail straight through the tossing waves and blowing winds of bad doctrine (Ephesians 4:14–16). The Ephesians 4 model does not imply an "executive board," American business style of church leadership, in which decisions are handed down to the membership from on high.

All this talk of community discernment raises a problem. Is the goal to be democratic, to take a poll of views in the church and go with the majority? No. Forming good doctrine is not about achieving popular consensus. God calls us to be a people set apart and often the popular consensus pulls us in the direction of the world and its values. The aim should be one of transformation, not accommodation, to be given the mind of Christ. In our society, privileging the majority is a real danger, which is why God has provided counterbalancing voices. Scripture is just such a voice. When we read the Bible with open hearts, it will often call us away from popular consensus, not towards it, and we need always to be open to its indictment against our biases. Given a chance to speak, our heritage will also raise questions about our trends and their motives. Furthermore, God provides the church with shepherds and teachers whose job it is to keep us from going astray.

How do we avoid giving in to popular consensus? By listening to these voices:

- voice of Scripture
- voice of tradition
- voice of our shepherds
- voice of the "prophet" in our midst

Nevertheless, at times the community does go astray, far astray, prompting God to raise up people who are like the Old Testament prophets, who rail against our complacency and error. We should be quick to listen to these teachers and preachers carefully, but not too quick to jump into their shoes. Scripture shows us that theirs is a lonely and difficult job, often marked by doubt and turmoil. Good "prophets" are confident, but not arrogant and self-righteous. They recognize their limitations and unworthiness and their love is for the life of the church, not their own rightness. Nor are they the sort of people who create personal followings for themselves.

Congregational Autonomy. The business of community discernment also raises questions about autonomy. Outsiders are typically fascinated by our stance on congregational autonomy. They wonder how you keep uniformity without central organization. The answer is. . . you don't. At least, not complete uniformity. Unless we're ready to accept an organizational structure and extra-congregational hierarchies of control, we'd better get used to diversity among our churches. We cannot claim biblical autonomy yet be intolerant of congregational diversity. That's like pulling the drapes closed then complaining that they block the sunlight. Given our emphasis on autonomy, we obviously hope that our churches will continue to find ways to stick together as a family, but we cannot expect completely uniform emphases and practices and styles. That uniformity has never really existed anyway. Nor should people in one congregation ordinarily feel a great burden for straightening out another congregation. On the rare occasion someone might feel justified in doing this, their judgment should be guided by core issues, not peripheral ones.

On the other hand, some churches are using the principle of autonomy as a license to disconnect from their heritage. Where people have known only the abusive misapplication of tradition, perhaps hostility to heritage is understandable. But they need to examine their motives carefully, asking questions like: Are we making decisions that favor maturity? Or are we being naïve about history? Are we yielding to reactive impulses or perhaps abdicating the control of our direction to foreign powers? Will our attempt to liberate ourselves result in our becoming enslaved to something ultimately harmful?

Tradition. We'd like to see churches develop maturity by encouraging an interest in their history and giving their tradition a clear voice in the process of doctrinal formulation. Giving tradition a voice doesn't mean insisting that things always remain the same. In fact, that would violate one of the strongest features of our heritage: the contention that we should repeatedly scrutinize the status quo in light of Scripture. Tradition is naturally conservative, resisting change, in a way. Yet deeply embedded within it is the dynamic of change and flexibility, because key traditions usually were developed at times of change and in response to need or crisis. A frank study of them often opens up channels of adaptability, suggesting creative alternatives for new situations. We should not be afraid that giving tradition a voice means surrendering to an entrenched norm.

If its authority is not that of unrelenting inertia or of unquestioning obedience, then what is the proper authority of tradition? We admit that this has always been difficult for Christians to pin down–so much so that the temptation to avoid dealing with it altogether is strong. It cannot be squeezed into an all-or-nothing template. On the one hand, we affirm that Scripture is our ultimate guide and that we should never put the tradition of our heritage on a par with Scripture. On the other hand, it's become apparent that

God works in our tradition somehow and that our tradition always affects how we read and apply Scripture, whether we consciously invite it to or not.

Giving tradition a voice means reserving a place for it at the table. It means identifying people among us who are especially interested in the story of our heritage and skilled in telling it, giving them the chance to do so and to contribute to decision-making processes in churches. It means yielding to the formative power of our story by trying our best to understand it sympathetically, seeing it through the eyes of those faithful people whose lives were part of the story. We should welcome the lessons it teaches us and praise God for his part in it. We should examinine our motives and maturity whenever we catch ourselves in knee-jerk reactions against tradition.

Sometimes we might bring a seemingly non-traditional proposal to the table, only to discover that it actually has strong parallels in our heritage and can be tied to some of our bedrock principles. Some angle out of the past may even enrich the proposal in ways we did not expect. At other times, bringing the proposal into a conversation with our heritage reveals some weakness in it that we had not considered. Or it helps explain someone's reaction to the proposal, negative or positive. The study may lead us to reevaluate our tradition carefully, perhaps finding a problem with it that we had never seen before. The exchange may be a positive one for innovation, or for tradition, or for both. Done well, it will be a positive gain for maturity in any case.

Both our heritage and the biblical text tell our story, the story of who we are. In that sense, tradition and Scripture fit together. The difference is that the Bible has the controlling story, the story by which our more recent narrative is to be measured and judged. Wherever the story of our heritage conforms to the account of Scripture, we can affirm that portion of our heritage as a further development of the biblical story, one that has been faithful to the intent of the author. We will also find points at which our story has not been faithful to the story of Scripture. At those places, we need to let God's Word reform us in order to avoid sectarianism that inevitably shatters unity on the altar of a self-confident false piety.

Perhaps our culture and language and situation have changed so that perpetuating a particular tradition unchanged would threaten to obscure or block the core of the scriptural story, either its content or its redemptive function. Then we seek to adjust the tradition in ways that let Scripture do its transformative work rather than hinder it. Even then, intentionally reading Scripture from within the context of our heritage may keep us from unwittingly adopting some other framework for reading it. If our tradition has little or no open voice in our Bible reading, then the sly voices emanating from our culture will take charge–voices beckoning us to read the Bible as a self-help manual, or as a tool for catching an emotional-spiritual buzz, or to find justification for any number of ministry schemes driven by the impulse to achieve measurable effectiveness.

As we said, the nature of the proper authority of tradition is difficult to pin down. Its authority is like that of a story told often and with passion. Few things have as much authority in the deep places of our hearts as the stories we constantly repeat. We want to plead the case of allowing the story of our heritage to be heard, repeatedly and everywhere. Doing so will shape a process of healthy doctrinal formulation in a church.

Deepening our Beliefs. One crucial task before us is that of appreciating the depth and richness of our own beliefs and practices and passing that appreciation on to others. Good doctrinal formulation is not about gathering lists of rules. Rules on a list tend to be equal to each another, possibly having little or no inter-connection. Their rationale and significance is just that of having been listed, nothing more. The list mentality is no good. Forming good, biblical doctrine involves more than tagging something with a "thus saith the Lord." Yet it also involves more than the default "approval" of Scripture's silence. Good doctrines take shape under the light of Scripture, but they emerge when we relate the topics together, arranging them around the core. Good doctrines have deep meaning, sometimes several, that the list mentality can scarcely touch. Healthy practice emerges as a lively synthesis, involving tradition and individual and communal relationships with the Lord, brought into dialogue with the Bible and hammered out on the front lines of ministry. Good doctrines invite us to plumb the depths of their meaning and connect it to our lives, using the imagination of Scripture to fill out their significance in as many ways as possible.

> Not long ago I was in England with a group of ACU students studying Christian worship. I introduced them to the Bishop of the local Eastern Orthodox Church, who talked with them about Orthodox worship. The students were stunned to learn that the Orthodox sing *a cappella* in their services; they'd assumed that Churches of Christ were the only ones with this peculiar habit.
>
> What really amazed them was the Bishop's rationale for the practice. He didn't merely stress the fact that this was the way the first Christians sang in worship. He also connected it to other things, including early Christian views of creation, their sense of our having been made by God's hands

> as the ideal worship instrument. He connected it to the Orthodox emphasis on unity as expressed in univocal singing and he stressed the priority of focusing solely on God in worship, without mechanical distractions. He referred to early Christian teachers on the subject. His goal was not to convince the students that *a cappella* worship was necessary for salvation, but to open their eyes to the *meaning* of this practice for Orthodox faith and devotion.
>
> It was obvious how rich and deeply precious this doctrine was to the Eastern Orthodox. Unfortunately, before this encounter the students had no idea that *a cappella* music in worship could have any other rationale beyond, "you're supposed to do it that way." Those who had accepted this rationale stuck by the essentiality of *a cappella* music, but had no deeper significance to rely on. Those who had rejected the rationale had presumed that it was just a matter of worship style or preference, to be altered on a whim if market pressures demand or tastes change. The Bishop's approach showed that both positions are shallow.
>
> *–Jeff*

There's certainly nothing wrong with doing a thing simply because God has commanded it. Parents of young children live by this principle–"Why, mommy?" "Because I said so!" But they also hope that one day their children will grow up and move beyond doing things only because they've been told to. They hope that their love for the lawgiver will lead them to embrace her will and explore its purposes more deeply!

To take one example, the New Testament connects the Lord's Supper to many different things–sacrifice, covenant meal, lifeblood, fellowship meal, marriage feast, thanksgiving, church unity, manna, the messianic celebration of heaven, and more. If we open up all its Old Testament connections, we get a picture bursting with meaning. Yet in some churches you will rarely hear the Lord's Supper linked with anything other than the one topic emphasized by Ulrich Zwingli during the Reformation, that of memorial.

We inherited this emphasis from Zwingli, and it is biblical, but it's only one piece of the multi-faceted picture with which Scripture wants to nourish us in the Supper. In some churches, even that lonely rationale is missing, when the Lord's Supper is conducted in such a way that the procedure seems to be saying: "We do this because we're supposed to." Here, bringing the story of our tradition alongside the story of Scripture would confirm our historical emphasis on the importance of weekly Lord's Supper and it would confirm the appropriateness of seeing it as a memorial. But it would also expose the historical source of our emphasis, challenging us to be even more biblical by exploring all the other rich associations communion has, letting them shape our language about it and our procedures for observing it, as some

Is it on the list?

One prominent Anglican Church, which traces its origins as a congregation back to the 10th century, recently remodeled its ancient building in order to build, among other things, an adult immersion baptistry. Very peculiar. Their Rector says, "it gives a reminder of the full significance of baptism.... We find that the drama of an adult baptism by immersion with words of explanation proves to be a powerful evangelistic tool."

It's ironic that we live in a time when a renewal of interest in practices like the Lord's Supper and baptism is occurring in many other groups who have not had the practices on their "list" but are drawn to the inherent biblical richness of the practices themselves.

In this climate, it will be sad if we have nothing more to say about our most cherished practices than that they are on the list of requirements. It will be doubly sad if we de-emphasize the practices out of a misguided notion of what it means to be oriented on grace.

churches are in fact doing. We have a strength here, but it can grow yet stronger.

One fear is that unless we focus on the commandment-nature of what we do, important practices will slip because we'll lose motivation to keep them. However, rule of law has never provoked the deepest motivation. In fact, searching Scripture only to find what is "necessary for salvation" is a minimalist approach that causes us to misconstrue much of Scripture's intent and cheats us of the abundant meaning of biblical doctrines.

One of the features common to the present generation is the quest for integrity and authenticity. They're looking for depth and for meaning. They will not value what we say is important just because we say so; they'll value what we value only when we prove to them how important it is to us and why, showing where it connects to our faith and our life. Our young people and most unchurched people are not impressed with the list rationale. Neither are they ultimately satisfied with eye-catching incentives that don't feed the soul. However, to the extent that we can weave our beliefs and practices into the fabric of Scripture and our heritage, and our own personal and corporate stories–and recount this saga in a way that invites these people to step into the story–they're hooked. The Apostles do this very thing in their deep exploration of a doctrine's significance, not just to hook the seeker, but because it is their natural way of thinking. Their spiritual sensitivities are perceptive of the wealth of interconnections between the deep things of God.

In practice, this means going well beyond the minimum in our study of the Bible's teachings. It means that we should meditate constantly on our doctrines and practices, exploring all the possible inter-connections between them, all the relevant reasons for them–spiritual, practical, emotional, whatever. It means gathering up the wealth of associations into the central images of the Christian faith: cross, baptism, Lord's Supper, etc. We should allow our reflections to permeate what is preached on Sundays and taught to our children and to converts. They should shape the way we conduct baptisms and our order of worship, how we craft mission statements, what forms of outreach we adopt, and the logo on the newsletter.

Deepening our beliefs is a *disciplined art*. Art pervades Scripture but is missing from much of our presentation and application of doctrine. Learning this art will help ensure that when we adopt forms and strategies engaging enough to bring people in from the outside, their meaning will not grow out of some secular agenda, but out of a reading of Scripture from the context of our heritage. This is what it means to develop the *discipline* of interpreting truth alongside the *art* of conveying it to people in a way that engages them at deep levels and compels them to sign on. In God's economy, neither truth nor the art of it should be compromised. Truth without elegance is untrue, or at least incomplete.

Connecting Beliefs to Behavior. Deepening our beliefs helps us explore how our doctrines and practices connect to our attitudes and lifestyles. The virtues required for good reading also tie in to healthy doctrinal reflection. Patternistic reading of the Bible and an overemphasis on institutional forms threatens to fracture our spirituality, disconnecting faith from morals. Too often Christianity has been boiled down to a procedure of checking public items off the list, while spirituality and lifestyle get little attention. When that happens, Christian morality is itself reduced to a set of rules, a list of the most obvious moral items, mostly drawn from culture. As culture and its morality have changed, we find ourselves unable to maintain moral ground when our ethics are not tied to the core of the Gospel story. Then grandparents wonder what went wrong with the youngsters who were so well tutored in the "basics" of the faith.

Whether we're talking about religious practices or moral behavior, we need to keep all of it connected together and centered on Christ. Feeding the homeless doesn't cancel out the need for sexual purity; nor does contributing money to the church somehow make up for neglecting our kids. Worshiping without an instrument does not excuse materialism; nor does religious rule-keeping provide the resources we need for moral living. Perhaps it's worth noting here that most of the time that a literal "thus saith the Lord" occurs in Scripture, it's in the Old Testament prophets, and usually tied to moral problems rather than external "religious" observances.

Paul usually mentions baptism and the Lord's Supper, not in contexts concerned with proper worship format, but when he's addressing moral issues (Romans 6:3–4; 1 Corinthians 10:16–21; 11:17–34; Galatians 3:26–29; Colossians 2:11–12). We need to figure out how to do this too. It shouldn't be difficult, since the Bible has a way of tracing threads of connection between doctrine, practice, and morals, by linking together concepts and images and language. The apostolic references to baptism and the Lord's Supper are profound examples, but the Bible contains many other models. When we cultivate doctrines deeply, probing their inter-connectedness, we discover that the Gospel lays a claim not only on our worship practices and our institutional forms, but also on our personal budgets, our career choices, our parenting styles, and how we choose to spend our time. For the true disciple, there are no separate categories. They are all owned by Christ. The stuff of good Christian doctrine touches them all.

Faith takes shape in life and in action. We can bind together Christian faith and lifestyle if we will use our preaching, teaching, and ceremony to connect the elements of faith and lifestyle to the story of Scripture and the story of our heritage.

Conclusion: An Ongoing Process

Sustaining a healthy process of doctrinal reflection is hard for any congregation to do. It would be much easier simply to let things go on as they always have, without question or scrutiny. For those wanting change, it would be easier just to rely on popular Christian resources for fresh insights and perspectives. Such outside resources can be stimulating and helpful, but using them is no substitute for owning up to the responsibility of doing the hard work of doctrinal reflection in every church.

Churches should intentionally design programs of doctrinal reflection, like Paul encourages Timothy and Titus to do. It is an ongoing process. From place to place and from age to age, the job of responsible reflection is never fully finished. It is especially necessary at critical times of change, or when circumstances arise that require major decisions and action, but it's wise to be in reflection at all times. A dynamic view of Christianity seeks constant growth and is always on the lookout for opportunities to mature further, aware that we have not yet arrived and are struggling to live up to what we have already attained (Philippians 3:12–16). Let's not succumb to the anesthetizing effects of patternistic reading, becoming victims of spiritual lethargy. We affirm the simplicity of the core

Gospel, but this affirmation is no excuse for failing to create within the church an exciting environment where we steadily pursue God's will in an ongoing process of maturing reflection that makes the soil of the congregation fertile for Christian growth.

Again, our aims in this book are to touch hearts and shape attitudes, not prescribe specific strategies. Specific strategies will arise only in specific situations. However, the following principles sum up our thoughts so far about healthy doctrinal reflection:

- Healthy doctrine begins with an attitude of trust in God.
- Healthy doctrine promotes and protects salvation, both in terms of eternal reward and as a complex, growing experience of the Christian life (individually and corporately).
- Church leaders should institute ongoing and intentional programs of doctrinal reflection.
- Church leaders should repeatedly examine existing beliefs and practices, along with proposed changes, in light of both Scripture and heritage. They should insist that any affirmation of the status quo or any proposed changes be connected deeply to Scripture and be related to heritage.
- Church leaders should explore the core of Scripture, checking to see that the core as they understand it governs the church's teaching, preaching, worship, ministry, and behavior.
- Church leaders should ensure that their members have a deep knowledge of Scripture and a basic, sympathetic understanding of their heritage.

- Church leaders should find ways to involve all their members in the process of reflecting on doctrine, pursuing programs of worship, education, and ministry that emphasize intergenerational connection.
- Church leaders should ensure that the teaching, preaching, and ceremony of the church enrich doctrine and practice and deepen the connection between faith and life.

Chapter 9

The Crux of the Matter

At this point I wanted to look away from the cross, but I did not dare, for I well knew that while I contemplated the cross I was safe and sound. Therefore I was unwilling to endanger my soul, for apart from the cross there was no safety...

–Dame Julian of Norwich, c. 1393

Crisis at Cityside Church of Christ

Sister Duncan had taken just about all she could. She had never gone to an elders meeting in her life, had never complained or criticized. She had been a faithful member of the Cityside Church for over forty years, twenty-seven with her husband, who was one of the church deacons, and the last thirteen as a widow. She went to Ladies' Bible Class every Thursday morning, served food every week to needy people with Meals on Wheels. She just wanted to be a good worker for the Kingdom, serving quietly and effectively. But she couldn't stay quiet any longer. She had just about had enough.

For the last four years, worship services have just gotten crazier and crazier–ever since the new youth minister, Kevin, was hired and was given the additional job of being the worship minister.

Kevin has been pushing for more and more change. Probably half the songs we sing are just youth songs.

You know, the kind of songs the kids sing at camp. Certainly not the reverent songs that God wants. There are no notes to these songs, just words up on a screen. Boys and girls in the youth group take turns each week running a little computer that projects the words up on a screen. It's hard to read, hard to follow, and many of us older folks just can't keep up. Some of my friends don't even sing any more. The whole thing is so frustrating.

One Sunday, after several of us complained, Kevin passed out song sheets with some of these songs, with the notes on them. Problem is, the younger people didn't even sing the songs the way they were written. The girls were singing these extra melodies. It was really distracting. You couldn't even sing harmony because the young folks were just singing all over the place. Why do we have to have all this? Why can't we just worship the way we used to?

Well, the situation got worse two Sundays ago. With hardly any warning, when Kevin went up to the stage, four other people went with him–two young men, two young women. They each had microphones and started singing like they were the stars of a show or something. I was flabbergasted. I couldn't even sing. They were closing their eyes, raising their hands. And two of them were women, for crying out loud. I couldn't worship God. Felt like a Pentecostal service broke out right in the middle of our church.

Kevin called them his "worship team." Said they were there just to fill in the harmonies, to help us sing. Well, they didn't help me and my friends sing. I couldn't even sleep that night. I've barely slept since. I used to be a member of a Church of Christ, but I don't think I am any longer. Something else has broken out in our building. It's certainly not the church I remember and love. I just don't think I can take it any more.

And so Sister Duncan prepared to share her frustrations with the elders. Six of her friends had come with her. Why had the elders let this happen to their church?

Robert Morgan was a young account executive in a local firm. He and Cindy had been at Cityside for the eight years since he had finished his MBA. The Morgans had both grown up in a Church of Christ, and had never considered being a part of any other group.

When they moved to town, they had wished there were more choices, but Cityside was really the only Church of Christ in town, so they pitched in and went to work. Their daughter was just beginning first grade and their son was in pre-school. And last year, the church asked Robert to be a deacon. But they had had misgivings for some time about the worship at Cityside.

Church is so dead compared to what we're used to. Sometimes it just seems right out of the old days. Until Kevin became the worship leader four years ago, every song seemed so old, so irrelevant. Can't we liven this up some? Does it have to be so boring every week? The Gospel isn't boring, it isn't irrelevant. Must our worship be?

Kevin has tried awfully hard to make things better, but there's not a lot he can do. We sing some of the songs that Cindy and I sang in college, but there's not enough of us who know them to do it well. And obviously, some of the members aren't into contemporary songs. They just sit there with their arms folded. The songs they want to sing are fine for THEIR generation. But why wouldn't they want us to sing songs that OUR generation likes?

I look at my two kids. They'd rather color and eat Cheerios for most of the service. The only time they perk up is when we sing one of the contemporary songs. But that hasn't been often enough.

I have several people at work that I have talked to about the Lord. I think they would be interested in going to church somewhere, but I'm embarrassed to invite them to Cityside. I don't think I could stand it. Somehow I think I'd have to apologize for a worship service that wouldn't connect with them at all.

It's not that the church isn't trying. A couple of weeks ago, Kevin introduced a worship team. It was a breath of fresh air, that's for sure. At least they're attempting to liven things up, make it relevant and engaging. But when all is said and done, it's probably too little too late. And it's obvious that more than a few people in the church are rising up to oppose it. I'm afraid we're getting ready to take a giant step backwards.

We've started visiting First Community Church up the block. It's not exactly what we're looking for, but at least the worship services are exciting. We don't want to leave Cityside. But if we keep on like this, we're likely to lose our children entirely. How can we get them to love the church when the church seems oblivious to what families like ours need? How can people like us invite our friends to come when it's obvious to them that we're miserable and know they would be too? What can we do?

We're not going to leave without talking to the elders, of course.

And so Robert and Cindy and three other couples slipped into the building and took seats in the waiting area next to Sister Duncan.

The situation at Cityside is essentially true, though the names and circumstances have been altered to guard the church's identity.

These brothers and sisters are members of the same church, attend the same worship service, and are lead by the same elders. What's a church to do?

The problems and how we are dealing with them vary from congregation to congregation. In some churches, issues such as the ones at Cityside aren't talked about openly but are whispered in hallways and at dinner tables. Others have lengthy study periods where elders and perhaps the whole church work through the issues so that they can try to agree on direction and purpose. In still others, there is public, occasionally angry, discourse. In many places, people just quietly leave and start worshipping elsewhere, largely unnoticed. And in a few tragic places, the church splits into two or more congregations, dividing friends and families and, surely, breaking God's heart.

To understand this crisis, we must remind ourselves again of the nature and function of *tradition*–the long-held and not-often-examined practices and rituals of the church. At Cityside, both Sister Duncan and Robert Morgan have certain understandings of what church ought to be like based on their own experiences. Each brings with them certain strongly held traditions. Both have valid concerns.

We must also have a sense of our own *history* so that we might understand what has driven our practices and our questions. Consciously or unconsciously, the individuals at Cityside are approaching this problem through the lens of the questions, issues, and practices of the Stone-Campbell Movement in North America, not only regarding the problem but how it is being addressed.

And it certainly is essential to look at *how we approach Scripture* so that we might address its issues in a healthy and appropriate way. We may all believe in the full authority of the Bible, but those who work to preserve the integrity of its historical and theological contexts have certain advantages in understanding its meaning and applications. But frankly, many of the issues at Cityside do not have precedent in Scripture. Both sides can cite passages. Both can argue from biblical examples. Both can claim the argument of scriptural silence.

Something else is needed, something that is the crux of the matter.

Wisdom and Power

Before we can address any of the issues at Cityside, we need to look at another church in another city. This is a church whose problems are beyond what most of us can imagine. Yet the solution for that community of believers provides the only answer that can possibly work for the kinds of problems our churches are facing in the opening years of the twenty-first century.

First-century Corinth had a reputation for debauchery and wealth, a kind of ancient New Orleans with money. It was a regional center of commerce and government. Though it couldn't compete with Athens just down the coast, it was also a place of culture and learning. And though only a few of the leading citizens had become Christians, several in the church had training in Hellenistic philosophy or brought into the church a Hellenistic worldview.

Some of them felt that their education and training allowed them to challenge the man who had established the church during his ministry there a few years before. They were appreciative of Paul but surely he had no real authority in relation to them now. He had not been trained in Greek philosophy. He had not been steeped in the literature of the great philosophical thinkers. His rabbinic training gave him certain advantages, perhaps, in relation to his fellow Jews. When it came to discussing Christian faith in the marketplace of Corinthian ideas, however, they felt Paul was somewhat disadvantaged. And since they prized both eloquence and erudition, Paul's apparent inadequacies in these areas certainly undermined his credibility with them.

They knew what Paul surely couldn't, that certain elements of the Christian message didn't play well in Corinth. It's not that they weren't important. They just needed to be toned down a little so that Corinthians wouldn't be turned off by them.

For example, Christians everywhere believe that Jesus of Nazareth was crucified. But that teaching was particularly difficult for Corinthians to swallow. Being executed as a criminal was a shameful thing, a source of embarrassment to many. That a god would become human and willingly be humiliated in this way just didn't make sense to a lot of people in Corinth. And add to that the notion of a bodily resurrection. The story was pretty bizarre.

If a person told the crucifixion and resurrection story to most of the Corinthian citizens, it would create a barrier to their becoming believers. It just wasn't effective evangelism. Better to keep that doctrine fairly low key. After all, Jesus taught many helpful things. Why not emphasize the teachings that touched people where they lived? It was just the smart thing to do.

This impulse toward *wisdom* as a touchstone for the Corinthian Christians was matched only by their concern for *power*. Their interest was not power in the sense of control or political manipulation. Rather, they saw themselves as people of the Spirit. They prided themselves in what the Spirit had given them, as manifested most clearly by the gift of tongues. And they were not sure Paul was such a person of the Spirit, with such power, at least not in the way and to the extent they were.

In fact, this pride in both wisdom and power appear to be connected. Their wisdom was itself a gift and was a demonstration of their being people of the Spirit. Whatever divisions there were among them–and there were several–they can't compare to their feelings of superiority in relation to Paul. They saw themselves as both wiser and more powerful than he.

When Paul wrote them an earlier letter, one we do not have, they did not respond well. They questioned his credibility and his authority. When he received their reply in a letter brought to him by Stephanas, Fortunatus, and Achaicus, it was clear that they were challenging his doctrinal positions, his prohibitions of certain behavior, and his credentials. It was in this context that Paul wrote his second letter, what we call 1 Corinthians.

Their pride in human wisdom, their lessening the role of the cross in Christian doctrine and their smugness about their spiritual power had led to certain consequences. Paul now systematically and quite candidly confronts them.

There were *divisions* in the church (chapters 1-4). Different groups, perhaps individual house churches, rallied around certain heroes–Paul, Apollos, Cephas, even Jesus, although those heroes were not party to the divisions. They openly *tolerated sexual immorality*, condoning in the name of enlightened tolerance a man who was having sexual relations with his stepmother (chapter 5).

They embarrassed the name of Christ and the cause of the church by *suing one another* in the law courts (chapter 6). Some of them were going into the city and *having sex with prostitutes* (chapter 6). Others were *abstaining from sex* with their own wives. (chapter 7). Some were *flaunting their freedom* by publicly buying meat at the marketplace that had been offered to idols and eating it, thus influencing weaker Christians to transgress their conscience and sin (chapters 8-10).

Their *worship services* had become a debacle. The Lord's Supper had become more about them than the Lord. It was a dividing instead of a uniting ceremony–rich against poor, one group against the other (chapters 10, 11). The tongue speakers and the prophets were arguing over which one had the more important gift (chapters 12-14). Some of the women, perhaps the wives of some of the prophets, were questioning their husbands in the assembly, disrupting the whole service (chapter 14).

And we think we have problems! Sometimes our issues seem large until we contrast them with churches who have real problems. Of course, as we experience them, our problems are quite painful, our upsets quite distressing, our difficulties quite real.

Resolved to Know Nothing...Except Jesus Christ and Him Crucified

As Paul addresses the Corinthians, he pulls no punches. The opening words make it clear who is in charge and reveal quickly where the problem lies. "Paul, called to be an apostle of Christ Jesus by the will of God..." In other words, "what I'm telling you is not of my invention, it comes from God. And *he* is the one who has sent me." Just a quick survey of the opening chapters reveals God as the subject and focus of sentence after sentence–

...it is the power of God...

...since in the wisdom of God...

...God was pleased...

...Christ the power of God...

...and the wisdom of God...

...God chose the foolish things of the world...

...God chose the weak things of the world...

...He chose the lowly things of this world...

...so that your faith might not rest on human wisdom but on God's power.

...we speak of God's secret wisdom...

...God has revealed...

...no one knows the thoughts of God...

In other words, *who do you think you are?* Do you think all this is about you, what you want, what you think is best, what you perceive as wise, who you think is smart? You have made decisions about how the church presents itself to the world so that your neighbors might be attracted to the message of Christ. But you have done it your way, by your own means, with your priorities. You have determined what you think is best, the message you think is most presentable.

You have grouped your little house churches so that you are only with people who are like you, who support your position, who see the Gospel your way. You humiliate the church and the cause of Christ by how you treat one another publicly. Privately, you act in your own interests. And in your assemblies, you exhibit selfishness and pettiness, the cause of Christ being subsumed under your own desires.

You think this is about you–your practices, your ideas, your wishes, and your presentation of the Gospel. But it's not about you at all. It is about God. It is about what *he* has done and what *he* now calls you to do. I come to you as God's apostle, bearing his authority, appealing to you with the same message I preached when I was with you.

By human wisdom, you think you know him, but you don't know him at all. God's foolishness is wiser than your wisdom. And what is wise to God, appears foolish to you. But nonetheless, that's what I proclaimed when I was with you. And it is still what you need to hear and do.

This is the essence of the Gospel: *Christ crucified.*

If you had lived out the implications of this Gospel, you wouldn't be in the predicament you're now in. If you lived a crucified life, you wouldn't be divided, group against group, gift against gift. You wouldn't tolerate blatant immorality in your midst, and you would protect the name of Christ and the mission of the church among the pagans.

If you lived a crucified life, you would recognize that what you do with your body matters, that it is the temple of God's Holy Spirit. You would realize that husbands and wives have responsibilities to one another, and that the concerns of God's Kingdom supercede them all.

The crucifixion carries implications about how you exercise your freedom. Sure, God does not forbid you to eat meat offered to idols. But if your exercising that freedom disrupts the church, if it creates a crisis which sullies the name of Christ and undercuts the ministry of the church, if, above all, it causes weaker Christians to lose their faith, then stop it! Christ gave up his freedom to serve you. He empowers you to give up your freedom to serve the church for his sake.

At all places and all times, let the power of his crucifixion change your assemblies. You come to church but instead of eating the *Lord's* Supper, you eat your own. You celebrate the death of Christ in the Supper while, in the very taking of it, you act as though Christ never died.

Here is the crux of the matter. The cross of Christ ought to make a difference in how you live, how you treat one another, how you restrain your freedoms and subdue your desires in order that others may be served. It ought to affect the choices you make, the words you use, the sacrifices you offer. The concerns of Christ should be reflected in everything you do.

Whenever you eat the bread and drink the cup, *you proclaim Christ's death.* His crucifixion transforms you from the inside out. It empowers you to embody the cross in your thoughts and in your behavior. The Supper is the very place where what I preached–Christ and him crucified–is enfleshed. The fact that your assemblies have become a place for your wishes to be carried out is an indication that you have not surrendered to the power of the cross and its consequences.

If you were living a crucified life, you would not be arguing as to which gift is greatest. But since you are, let me tell you. The gift of prophesy–speaking a word from the Lord to the church–is a more important gift than tongues. But neither of them can compare to the gift of love. All the other gifts will ultimately go away. Only love will remain.

In the name of Christ, then, don't allow your assemblies to be a free-for-all. Let your speech be understandable so that the whole church is built up. If unbelievers are present while this happens, they might understand the Gospel, the secrets of their hearts being laid bare. And, perhaps, they might even join the surrender of lives taking place there, declaring with the saints, “Surely God is in our midst.”

When you come together, each of you is attempting to do your own thing, whether bringing a hymn or a word of instruction, a revelation, a tongue or an interpretation. Don’t allow these to become expressions of your individual wishes. Rather exercise these gifts to build up the whole church. And if the prophets’ wives must challenge their husbands, let them do so at home where it will not disrupt the worship and the service of the saints.

Above all, remember the Gospel by which you were saved. What I received from the Lord is what I preached to you. It is of first importance, before anything else be considered or done, that Christ died for our sins according to the Scriptures, that he was buried, that he was raised on the third day according to the Scriptures, and that he appeared to more than 500 people. And he appeared to me also. This is what I preached. This is what you first believed. Live like it.

Live anticipating your own resurrection, the resurrection of your spiritual body, raised with Christ after his death, sharing in his victory over yours. And don’t forget to give to those who are in need. I will be looking for your generous gift to Christians in poverty. They need your help. I will look forward to receiving your contributions for their sake when I come.

Hellenistic wisdom does not lead to this kind of generosity. Exercising your power does not call you to these kinds of sacrifices. This kind of living does not come from you. It is only a gift from God. It may not seem wise for the Son of God to be humiliated on a Roman cross, and it may appear to be quite weak for him to have died there, but nevertheless it is God’s wisdom and God’s power. It is the Gospel by which you are called to live.

This is the message of 1 Corinthians in its essence, chapter by chapter. It is the message of the cross in its fullness, with all its demands, in all its power, with all its hope. We can deal with nothing else until this issue is addressed. It is of first importance. The future of the church is at stake. It is the crux of the matter, both for the Corinthians and for us.

The Shadow of the Cross in Churches of Christ

We probably don't identify too much with the tendency of the Corinthian Christians to underplay the cross. After all, we talk about it quite a bit. We wear little gold crosses around our necks and display them on the bookmarks of our Bibles. Some of us even decorate our homes with them. Our assemblies are peppered with the language of crucifixion. Surely our hymnody reveals its prominence. "At the cross, at the cross, where I first saw the light." "Beneath the cross of Jesus, I fain would take my stand." "O sacred head now wounded with grief and shame weighed down." Hymn after hymn reveals the place of the crucifixion of Christ in our

"I CAME TO HEAR SOMETHING NEW"

A couple of years ago, after one of the authors finished a three-part series on the crisis of identity in Churches of Christ and spoke of the place of the cross in our renewal, one preacher was quite critical afterwards. "I came to all three hours expecting to hear something new."

But the solution to our problems does not lie in something new. That's precisely what the Corinthians were proposing. It was not a new word that they needed to hear. Rather it was the one they first believed when they were converted by the preaching about a crucified Christ.

During this crisis at the beginning of the twenty-first century, our future lies in whether or not we will immerse our conversations and our thoughts, our churches and our hearts, in the cross of Christ.

doctrine. We certainly are not embarrassed about the shame of the cross. Besides, since we insist everyone be baptized, how could the cross be diminished? We believe baptism is the place where we are washed by the blood of Christ. Of all groups, surely ours would not be one where the cross was diminished or ignored.

Interestingly, when Bill Love examined the place of the cross in the Stone-Campbell tradition during the writing of his seminal book, *The Core Gospel,* he discovered how little it was referred to in books and sermons for most of two centuries. In the first generation, Stone, Campbell and their peers, assumed certain beliefs about the cross. Most of their followers had emerged from Presbyterian and Baptist churches. They shared a Reformed view of Christ and the crucifixion, largely Calvinist in influence. There were few differences among these preachers concerning the place of the cross in Christian doctrine, so they mostly discussed and wrote about other matters. While Stone and Campbell occasionally expressed their view of the cross and its place in Christianity, it was not prominent in their preaching because almost everyone they knew already agreed with them.

By the second generation of the Restoration Movement, however, neither shared beliefs of the Christians nor common views of the preachers concerning the crucifixion of Christ could be assumed. Nevertheless, it continued to be a topic largely ignored in the public discourse among church leaders. Printed sermons rarely mentioned it. Books summarizing the first principles of the church referred to it little, if at all. It certainly found no place of prominence in the disputes of the last years of the nineteenth century which led to the division between Churches of Christ and the Christian Church/Disciples of Christ.

Throughout the difficulties and divisions of the twentieth century, whether over pacifism during World War I, pre-millennialism, having Sunday Schools, using only one cup in the Lord's Supper, cooperative congregational support of orphans homes, constructing fellowship halls, meeting in cell churches, handclapping, or using choruses or worship teams in the assembly, there seems to have been little mention of the cross, either in sermons or conversations about these issues. It has rarely appeared to have much effect either on our content or our behavior, no matter how much we may have sung about the cross or how prominently it may have been displayed on our bodies and in our churches and homes.

Obviously, there are significant exceptions. Love, in his book, mentions a trend toward the end of the twentieth century for the cross to find its place again in the pulpits of our churches. But our history is checkered at best in this regard. We may need the message of 1 Corinthians more than we know.

It seems a bit self-evident to say that the cross should be at the center of Christian living. It's like saying learning should be at the heart of education. But nothing so patently obvious can be assumed, as many students and teachers can testify. To say, redundantly, that the crucifixion of Jesus is the crux of the matter is bound to spawn yawns among some readers. But there is no other Gospel than this, no other foundation, no other solution.

The Cross and Views of Biblical Authority. It is not enough to have the right views about the nature and function of Scripture. We believe with all our hearts that the Bible is fully inspired and authoritative for everything we do. In spite of some rhetoric to the contrary, almost everyone in Churches of Christ believes this. There are differences in understanding the nature of

Scripture, to be sure. This we have already discussed. But whether Scripture is the authoritative Word of God is not a disputed matter.

However, a person can believe in the full inspiration of Scripture and still not speak and act as a person changed by the cross of Christ. Almost every day there are people who slander and malign fellow Christians, accuse and undercut their ministries, label them as "liberal" or "conservative," write them up as a dangerous or false teachers, dismiss them as uneducated or ill-informed, or gossip about them, saying things that are never said to their faces. These actions are done not because people don't believe in the Bible. They do. These things are said not because their "hermeneutic" is old or new, right or wrong. Issues of biblical interpretation must be discussed, but this is not what is creating these inappropriate behaviors. Something else is missing, something closer to the heart of the matter.

Some editors of papers and journals among Churches of Christ use language in virtually every issue that no secular newspaper or magazine would tolerate. Branding certain ministers or teachers, impugning their motives, making accusations, heaping ridicule upon people whom they have not met, with whom they have never prayed. And all of it is done in the name of proclaiming the Word of God.

Our public communication must be immersed in the blood of Christ. Our articles, editorials, and sermons must come under the scrutiny of the cross. We must be willing to take literally Jesus' injunction of Matthew 18 to visit those who we feel have sinned against us and to pursue the spirit of this passage even regarding those with whom we may simply disagree. To say that we have the right to print criticisms against other people because they are public figures and deserve to be criticized is attempting to apply human wisdom when divine wisdom is in order. Even pagan editors have higher standards, if only to avoid the lawsuits that Christians are still unlikely to file. It is time to stop calling this type of communication "conservative." It is not conservative because it does not flow from the biblical witness. It runs counter to it. It is not cross-shaped communication, whatever the motives of its contributors and editors.

We must take seriously Paul's last exhortations to Timothy to correct, rebuke and encourage with great patience and careful instruction. Even those we oppose must be treated with gentleness. Like Paul, we must declare an end to quarrelsome behavior and foolish arguments and instead fill our churches with healthy teaching. This is what the cross demands, wherever else human wisdom may lead us.

But just as some of us err in the ways we condemn people we disagree with, others pride themselves in how tolerant they are. They don't want to be known as small-minded and judgmental. They are embarrassed by the rhetoric of exclusivism. In their reaction to such abuses, they run headlong towards the god of tolerance. Don't make people uncomfortable, they say. Everyone has a right to their opinion, to their lifestyle. As a result, for some, expectations for Christian living and discipleship are quite low. There is too little concern for accountability, too few occasions for the kind of discipline we see evidenced among the first-century churches.

> I visited with a friend who had decided to leave his wife and children because he wanted to move in with his lover. He and I talked about the place of appropriate church discipline in this situation. He kept telling me, "The church ought

> to just love me. They should just tell me how much they love me. Why do you have to judge?"
>
> I asked him if there would ever be a situation where the church might discipline a member, and he said no. I gave him a hypothetical situation. "What if a member were having sexual relations with his stepmother? Do you think it would be appropriate or responsible for the church to say he should not live that way, and that if he didn't stop, the church would sever it's fellowship with him?"
>
> "Absolutely not," he said.
>
> I said, "Now understand me. I don't mean the church would disfellowship him as a form of punishment but in order to indicate that this is outside the bounds of appropriate Christian behavior, that he's doing so willfully. So the church is calling that person back to the values of Christ."
>
> He said, "He should not be disfellowshipped. People should just surround him with love."
>
> I told him, "But do you understand that the hypothetical situation I just told you about is from Scripture itself? From 1 Corinthians 5? And Paul made it clear that the person should be appropriately disciplined, both for his sake and the church's sake."
>
> He just shrugged his shoulders. "Well, I think Christians should just love one another."
>
> *–Jack*

The view this friend expressed is actually shared by more than a few church members. Some believe we should never tell people in the church what to do. To love means being tolerant of others' behavior; disciplining anyone is to judge them. But this lack of regard for appropriate Christian behavior and discipleship not only misunderstands Jesus' command against judging, it runs counter to the claims of the cross. Paul's letter to the Corinthians, rooted in the crucifixion of Christ, calls for a different kind of behavior–both for the ones living in immorality and for the community of believers to whom they are accountable. For the same reason that we should not slander people, sullying their names and reputations in order to press our own agendas, so we should not, in the name of tolerance, accept the behavior of Christians whose lifestyles and decisions undercut the cause of Christ and damage the effective ministry of the church. Neither behavior is cross-shaped. Neither lives out the implications of Christ's crucifixion.

The Cross and Restoration. Most of us in Churches of Christ have made a great point about restoring the practices of the New Testament. We are participants in a Restoration Movement and believe in its ideals. But it is not enough to try to restore the form of New Testament Christianity if we do not attempt to restore its heart.

We can have the right church organization, design the right worship service centered around the right acts of worship, and wear the right name and still not restore the church Christ died for. Thousands of people go to church every Sunday at congregations throughout our Movement who have made no real commitment to be Christ's disciples and have made no changes in light of the demands of the cross, however much they may enjoy the worship. In the Fifties and Sixties, dozens of preachers at churches whose worship practices bear all the marks of our restoration preached against racial integration and participated in racist practices, all in the name of Christ, without any recognition that the practices were un-Christian and sinful. Today, many churches would never allow individuals to clap or raise their hands during a worship service or accept as a member a person who has been divorced, but would not discipline a person for being materialistic, telling a racist joke, humiliating their wife at home, ignoring the poor, or neglecting their aging parents.

It's not enough to restore the form of the church if it doesn't lead to changed behavior. Paul warned Timothy about those who would have a form of godliness but deny its power (2 Timothy 3:5). This is certainly true for the kinds of people listed there: lovers of themselves, lovers of money, boastful, proud, abusive, disobedient to their parents, etc. It is also true for those of us whose restoration of the New Testament is focused on what our churches look like, how they are organized, or how much freedom we have when we worship. These are important issues and should be addressed in our churches. But unless Christians understand the implications of the cross, until they are willing to act as cross-shaped people in their service and surrender, whatever gains may be made will be hollow. Concerns for such things as form and organization, freedom and giftedness have meaning only after we've faced the crux of the matter. This is the heart of restoration–and the Gospel.

A Resolution for Cityside

With this in mind, what advice should be given to the leaders of the Cityside church? How can this crisis be resolved without people leaving or the church splitting? The issues are not simple. We would be audacious to claim we knew exactly how to handle it. Much depends on the personalities of the individuals and the complexities of the situation.

Moreover, in large measure the issues we have addressed in this volume have been designed more to cultivate a different attitude than to provide a program of response. Most of us, of course, are anxious to get to solutions. That's understandable and desirable. We should not be too quick, however, to move to answers when time is needed to right the heart. Many of us short-circuit our time in the wilderness in the name of being practical. Years of spiritual immaturity in the name of pragmatism is no replacement for the hard work of character development and spiritual discernment.

But some things can be said. First, the views of both Sister Duncan and Robert Morgan have been shaped by the tradition of the church. Sister Duncan's is perhaps easier to see. The way worship had been done at Cityside church–the order of worship, the types of songs, the placement of communion, the words of the prayers–these have been the norm for decades. She had never known a situation in which church was done differently, so it is difficult for her to separate such things as style of music and its presentation form (with musical notations) from her sense of what is the essence of worship. Like most of us, she would have a hard time imagining a Jewish-Christian worship service in first century Jerusalem or house church worship with one of the groups in Corinth. In both of these places, the assembly would hardly be recognizable to most of us, yet the essence of their worship was the same as ours. Sister Duncan's tradition of worship, rooted in early-and mid-twentieth century America, is powerful in its effect on her and meaningful for her Christian walk. She's right not to discard it casually. But its form is at least as modern as it is ancient. Its decades-long practice in the church does not give it the weight of Scripture.

On the other hand, Robert Morgan stands, perhaps unconsciously, in the tradition of free churches, which believe no set liturgical patterns should be imposed. To Robert, doing worship the same way all the time, especially as the services reflect the preferences and styles of previous eras, is not just aggravating, it's dangerous. A church must adapt its style to each generation or it will lose its voice and its reason for existence. It must not allow congregational lethargy or inattentiveness to prevail. Moreover, Robert believes the majority of worshippers should not be held hostage by the opinions and preferences of the minority, a view rooted not only in Free Church tradition but in American individualism and democracy.

For both Robert and Sister Duncan, their perspectives on what should be done are deeply affected by the tradition in which they both stand, though neither of them is very conscious of it. Wise leaders will help each of them come to grips with the baggage of tradition they bring to the table, not so that it might be discarded, but so that it might be unpacked and understood. Both perspectives have merit; both have blind spots regarding the other. For each of them, perhaps, a clearer grasp of the power of tradition might help them see how their points of view have been shaped not only by Scripture but by the way they and their spiritual ancestors have come to view church. More importantly, they might come to have a renewed appreciation for the feelings and experiences of the other. Wise leaders will take the time to come to grips with issues of tradition.

Second, all the participants in this tense situation stand firmly within the heritage of restorationism. In this, there are both obstacles and avenues to resolution. On one hand, our heritage in the Stone-Campbell Movement reminds us that we are often pre-occupied with forms–with how things look on the outside. Other restoration groups emphasized different things. The Swiss Anabaptists, for example, the predecessors of the modern-day Mennonites, were more concerned with restoring New Testament piety than patterns.

For us, however, getting the structure, organization, name, and form has been at the forefront of our discussions. This certainly functions as a powerful fuel in the Cityside situation.

Moreover, this focus on form has contributed significantly to the assumption of many that all Christians should look alike, that all assemblies should be alike. In other words, we take "being of like mind," using a familiar expression of the Apostle Paul, to mean uniform practices and beliefs. If the elders at Cityside assume that with proper pastoral care, the Morgans and Sister Smith will come to complete agreement on how worship should be done, they might as well brace themselves for an escalation of the problem. The likelihood is high that the Morgans would leave and find a place more compatible with their views. And if the Morgans get their way, Sister Duncan is likely to be unhappy until the day she dies.

On the other hand, within the restoration heritage is a strong thread of unity within diversity. The uniting of people who do not see eye to eye or practice their Christian faith identically was woven into the fabric of our history. Because we have not been very faithful in passing on these stories of our past, the part of our tapestry displaying unity within diversity is often not very visible, or it is marginalized. Perhaps this is a time to tell the stories of our heritage, to remind us of where we came from, of how people of considerable disagreement were able to worship together and love one another. As messy as such an arrangement is, it's far superior to forcing people to choose or to leave. It may mean neither of the participants will get their way totally, that the assemblies will reflect the wishes of both. There will be no victors in such a situation–except for the church. And Christ.

Third, no solution to a situation like that at Cityside is possible without a serious appeal to Scripture. But it must be an approach to Scripture that does service to how the Bible functions, that reflects its intent and its desired effect. This is no time to rummage through the text looking for individual verses ripped out of their literary and historical contexts, attempting to shore up the defenses of each position. Nor is it a time to claim that the Bible is just a collection of love letters giving general guidelines for our day, but that we really have the freedom to do mostly what we want.

In our brief foray through 1 Corinthians, we made a serious attempt to make the argument as Paul made it, to allow each verse to fit into the literary whole, to see the content of the letter out of the backdrop of specific historical issues which caused Paul to write the letter in the first place. It was done with respect for Paul's overriding theology, making sure each conclusion was not contradicted by other teachings within the epistle, or the rest of Paul's letters, or the witness of Scripture as a whole.

We make no claims this was done flawlessly. The problems are immense. For example, we do not know for sure how great the hostility was between the Corinthians and Paul, whether it was isolated to a few leading members or reflected the feelings of the whole church. It's hard to say exactly what was going on among the groups claiming allegiance to Paul, Apollos, Cephas, or Christ. The cultural context in Corinth which led Paul to urge women to wear a head covering certainly complicates our understanding of the message in chapter 11, not to mention Paul's mysterious statements that this should be done "because of the angels." No wonder even Peter found Paul difficult to understand!

But this does not cause us to throw up our hands in resignation. It calls for careful study, the examination of words and how they were used in the first century and in the rest of the New Testament. It demands theological discernment and an ability to see each part in relation to the whole. And, most importantly, it throws us before Scripture in humility. Fruitful Bible study does not grow out of arrogant presumption before the text but out of prayerful, pious surrender. Difficult passages, such as several in 1 Corinthians, remind us that we do not know everything, that God is still in charge, and that we must devote ourselves to a lifetime of looking and listening.

Significantly, we do not approach the text as lone strugglers and searchers. We live and work in a community of believers. The church is the primary medium through which healthy interpretation will occur. Eccentric readings can be honed. Selfish interpretations can be filtered through the activities of service and sacrifice. Those who have particular expertise in language, history, or proclamation can assist the church in her understandings, but never in authoritarian or controlling ways. People devoted to prayer can infuse the church with a commitment to purity and a keener dependence on the God who still works in our midst. These are potent forces to bring to bear in a situation such as Cityside faces. The message of Paul in 1 Corinthians and the overall message of Scripture as it is mediated through the community of faith will be critical in helping resolve the conflict and lower the tensions.

All of that said, the overriding message of 1 Corinthians is clear, and it has immediate application to the situation at Cityside. The leaders of this church must call all the participants back to the cross. Only here can attitudes be changed and hearts opened. Out of the experience of the cross comes the discipline to live rightly and the grace to love boldly.

The problems in this congregation should not be resolved primarily on the basis of arguments related to the surface-level issues. At some point, of course, these must be discussed. But something else must happen first, for Sister Duncan and her friends, for the Morgans and theirs, for Kevin, and for the elders. The cross of Christ demands certain behaviors and certain attitudes. It affects how we judge people who are different from us. It calls for us to give up some things we like, including the freedom to do whatever we want. It demands that we look out for the interests of others rather than our own.

Such an outlook does not call us to abandon our view of Scripture. It doesn't call us to compromise our convictions. But it does call for us to listen, to be slow to criticize and judge, quick to encourage and help. It doesn't easily answer the dilemma the Morgans face concerning the disconnectedness their children are beginning to feel from church. But it does tell them what they must teach their children, not only about people like Sister Duncan and her friends, but about doctrines that connect their kids to the cross of Christ.

At one level, our heritage may not help us as much as we want in this regard. We have not talked about the cross enough over the years. For that reason, our history is littered with quarrels, pettiness, and division. If the crucifixion of Christ is not at the center of our current conversations, if it does not change both the people and the content of the discussions, the result will be the same. We've been here before. We know how the story ends. At the same time, if we look for them, we will find in our past heroic stories of sacrifice and grace, of forbearance and compassion. Now is the time for these stories within our churches to be told and modeled for ourselves and the generations to come.

Divisions are not inevitable, even at the dawn of a new, confusing, postmodern world. God has presented us with a wonderful opportunity. He has given us all we need to negotiate these difficult shoals. Whatever else it will take, what we most need is to preach and live the crucified Christ, displaying it every day until Christ comes. The future of our churches depends on it.

Chapter 10

The Future of Churches of Christ

Be still my soul; thy God doth undertake
To guide the future as He has the past.
Thy hope, thy confidence let nothing shake;
All now mysterious shall be bright at last.
Be still, my soul; the waves and winds
still know
His voice who ruled them while
He dwelt below.

–Katharina von Schlegel, 1752

There is Something About a Wall

Our families sat in the grass on the downwind side of the wall, away from the gusts that howled over the tops of the stones. The Childers, Foster, and Reese families, along with a dozen graduate students together for a five-week stint in England, rendezvoused at the base of Hadrian's Wall near the ruins of a look-out post and barracks on the south side. We sat for a while, imagining what it was like for the Roman soldiers who were garrisoned there almost two thousand years before.

In A.D. 122. the Emperor Hadrian visited Britain and determined that an ongoing Roman campaign against the Picts, who were hiding in the mountainous terrain of Caledonia, was too costly. Nor was it possible to introduce them to the Roman way of life. While the Romans could easily defeat them in battle, it would be difficult to totally subjugate them. So Hadrian built a wall separating the barbarians from the Romans, establishing the northern boundary of Britain. The wall, extending 80 miles from the Irish Sea in the west to the North Sea in the east, protected the Roman citizens–the British–from danger from the outside.

As we sat in the shadow of the wall, we could almost hear the bark of orders and the pounding hearts of Roman soldiers standing on the fortification just above, peering into the northern wilderness, braced for a sudden attack.

With only a few breaches over the centuries, Hadrian's Wall was a symbol of Romano-British power over their less-civilized neighbors. But in the end, it was not enough. At the close of the fourth century, Britain was overrun by the Picts from the north, the Scots from Ireland who invaded western Britain, and the Saxons from Northern Europe who invaded from the south and east.

The problem had nothing to do with the wall. It was well fortified and strong, having withstood almost three centuries of barbarian attacks. The demise of Britain was occurring over a thousand miles away, well off British soil, across the channel and in the heart of the Continent.

The citizens who lived near the wall grew increasingly frantic during the last days. If the Romans would just pour more matériel, send more soldiers, give more attention to what was happening at the wall, surely it could be re-fortified. But the soldiers never came. Rome crumbled from the inside out, beginning with its capital and moving out to the frontier. Because it was not strong at the center, what happened at its outer fringes hardly mattered in the big picture of things. When the Visigoths sacked Rome in 410, Roman Britain had already met its end.

By the time our three families stood on top of the wall gazing across the barrenness, the terrors that had happened there sixteen centuries before were only a distant memory.

The demise of Roman Britain serves, perhaps, as an apt metaphor for the crises we face in twenty-first-century Churches of Christ. The parallels are tenuous, of course, but surely they stand as a reminder that what happens at the center dramatically affects what happens at the edge. If Rome had not crumbled from the inside out, British history would have been far different. No matter how much attention was given to the borders of the Empire, when the center collapsed, nothing was left to sustain the rest.

This is why we must not be distracted by matters on the edge when the times call for us to re-focus on the crux of the matter. And frankly, at times the history of Churches of Christ has reflected too much energy aimed at the margins, too many troops garrisoned at the periphery, too little attention to the center of things. This must not be such a time.

At the Cross

We have attempted to describe the crises that many of our churches are facing. Crisis in worship, crisis in leadership, crisis in behavior, and mostly crisis in identity. Some of the issues are about painful but nevertheless peripheral matters, in our opinion. Others, we believe, are at the heart of things. Distinguishing between the two will be among the greatest challenges Churches of Christ will face in the next several decades. It will determine where we will invest our spiritual and intellectual resources and ultimately whether this fellowship will have a voice and a witness in the third millennium.

Many of the things that have divided Churches of Christ over the past two centuries have not been *crucial* matters–that is, issues and practices directly tied to the cross of Christ. This is not to say that these matters were not important or should not have been discussed. Issues such as Christian pacifism and premillennialism, lively topics of discussion early in the twentieth century, are important topics of conversation. But they are not at the crux of things. They are important skirmishes on the boundary but are not critical for the defense of the capital.

Of course, these issues are not so divisive 75 years later. They are rarely topics of conversation among our churches today. Most of us have little emotional involvement in them. But this is not the case concerning the issues that led to our separate identity from the Christian Church/Disciples of Christ, churches which share our Stone-Campbell heritage. Not having missionary societies and using only *a cappella* music in our assemblies have served as identifying marks of our fellowship for a hundred years. These can hardly be discussed, even a century after the great split, without emotion and even tears. But however important these may be to our self-identity, they are not at the crux of the matter either.

We should be clear about this. We are advocates of neither missionary societies nor instrumental music. Concerning the latter, which has become a topic of vigorous conversation in some quarters over the last ten years, we believe there are a number of grounds for affirming *a cappella* singing in our churches–some theological, some historical, some practical. The three authors have each been outspoken proponents of *a cappella* music and have urged church leaders not to introduce instruments into worship. But it is not at the crux of things. Its practice is not tied to the crucifixion and resurrection of Jesus. Nor is it an issue ever addressed in Scripture, either explicitly or implicitly. We are unwilling to make Scripture mean what it could not possibly have meant in its original context. In fact, genuine biblical conservatism demands that issues such as this, which were not a concern for the first-century churches, should not become a litmus test for orthodoxy or grounds for disfellowship in our own day. This topic will be explored much more fully in a later volume in this series.

We recognize how volatile topics such as this can be. Recently, Jack publicly quoted a man who sincerely believes that handclapping in our assemblies is a far more significant issue than the worldwide AIDS epidemic. Implied, of course, was Jack's questioning of that assertion. In reply, an earnest brother made clear his opinion that handclapping, as well as raising hands, women leading in worship, and fellowshipping denominations, are doctrinal issues not matters of opinion. He asked, "How many souls can AIDS destroy? How many can be destroyed by false doctrine?" Since handclapping does not have a "thus saith the Lord" in the New Testament, it is therefore false doctrine, and its prohibition must be among the fundamentals of the faith.

We respect the right of this brother to believe that non-handclapping is a first principle of Scripture, the violation of which would cost a person their salvation. We uphold his right to express this view clearly and publicly. But from our understanding of Scripture, this will be a hard case to make for at least two reasons. First, those insisting on a "thus saith the Lord" for every practice will be hard pressed to be consistent. Contemporary churches do many things for which there is no biblical command or precedent–youth ministers, church buildings, pews, pulpits, song books, Sunday School, church secretaries, chairmen of the elders, bulletins, and missions committees. (This is not to mention practices where there is, in fact, a "thus saith the Lord" but which we do not practice in our churches, such as washing feet, greeting one another with a kiss, and men raising holy hands in prayer.) While expressing such concerns does great honor to the commitment we all have to place ourselves under the authority of Scripture, it ultimately does disservice to the force and intention of Scripture itself, as we discussed in chapters 7 and 8.

Second, and most importantly, as emotionally-laden as such issues as clapping hands in church may be, they do not lie at the crux of the matter. They do not emanate from the cross of Christ. They are certainly issues that need discussion, but they should not be issues that divide our churches. We believe such a practice falls within the Christian freedom Paul describes in 1 Corinthians. But because it is a freedom, it may be given up for the sake of the church if it causes people to sin, destroys their faith, or divides a church (not just because some don't like it). This is what it means to be "all things to all people"–relinquishing freedoms for the sake of the body. In some churches, its practice would be unwise at best and selfish at worst. Our behavior in such instances must be cross-shaped. Our response in such matters *is* at the crux of things.

There are some doctrines and practices, of course, which are non-negotiable. They do not lie at the frontier but in the capital. They emanate from the very person of Christ. They are directly tied to his teachings, his ministry, his crucifixion and resurrection, and they must be proclaimed with boldness. Among them are these:

We believe in baptism of believers by immersion for the forgiveness of sins. Baptism is not a human work, but the work of God; it is not merely a step of salvation but the place where the divine actions of justice and mercy encounter the human need for righteousness and grace. No salvation is possible other than through the blood of Christ–the washing of our sins by his work in baptism, our sharing in the power of his death and resurrection, and our receiving of his Holy Spirit as a gift. To proclaim the essential nature of baptism is not to deny the sovereignty of God, as if it makes salvation dependent on human works. On the contrary, baptism proclaims God's sovereignty, denying the independence and merit of humans. To say, for example, that baptism is an important result of salvation, like reading the Bible faithfully or finding a church home, is to make baptism precisely what it must not be–a human work. Moreover, to do so is to indicate that salvation comes through human response rather than the blood of Christ. Baptism proclaims that we cannot save ourselves; only Christ can. It would be hard to imagine a Christian doctrine or practice closer to the crux of the matter than this.

We believe that encountering the cross of Christ in baptism leads to changed behavior in the world. What Christ accomplished at the cross is carried out in our sacrificial living for his sake. Our baptism is the gateway for God's empowerment of holy living–the control of our tongues, the gentleness of our behavior, our commitment to serve the weak, our pledge to place others ahead of ourselves, our desire to relinquish control over our own lives, our willingness to surrender our time and possessions for the Kingdom's sake.

We believe our commitment to be holy and Christ-like in every thought and action both grows out of and feeds our yearning for God in such things as worship, study, and prayer. Christ's sacrifice on the cross draws us to thanksgiving and praise, forces us to our knees in surrender, compels us to repentance, and quickens our desire to know Him more and listen to him more attentively. It propels us to a life of prayer and a keen discernment to God's leading.

We believe the implications of the cross are most visible within the community of believers–the church. The church is the expression of Christ's body, his ongoing incarnation, the suffering presence of Christ on earth. Following Christ simply as individuals is not possible. We are drawn together as a community of witnesses of the cross and resurrection of Christ. We are recipients of his power, calling the world to be reconciled to Him, proclaiming the message of the cross, serving others in his name, bearing his marks, caring for his creation, living out his mission. In short, all of Christ's purpose and power are invested in his body, the church. A robust doctrine of the nature and work of the church will always be at the crux of the matter.

We believe our weekly participation in the Lord's Supper serves as an ongoing covenant to be people of the cross. The importance of our taking the bread and the cup each week reflects much more than mere compliance to apostolic example. Jesus says we partake of the Supper *in remembrance.* The Hebrew notion of remembrance is foreign to most westerners. It means that a past event is not just recalled but re-experienced. For Jews, Passover is a re-participation in the events of the exodus, not just a distant recollection. For Christians, the Lord's Supper is a re-experiencing of the cross. The power that caused the earth to shake and blackened the sky, the power that caused every sin committed from the beginning of creation to the end of time to be laid on Christ's shoulders, the very power that rolled the stone away and breathed life into his dead body is re-experienced again by Christians as we eat the bread and drink from the cup. And in so doing, we accept the covenant of God to be his people, to receive forgiveness of sins, and to show Christ's death in the way we live until he comes. And, as the early Christians did, we celebrate each Lord's Day because it is the day Jesus rose from the grave–the crucifixion and resurrection being intimately connected in the life and worship of the church.

Each of these issues is crucial, each of them calls us away from skirmishes at the frontier and back to the capital, each of them stands at the crux of the matter.

Crisis, Tradition, and the Future of Churches of Christ

Much of our discussion in this volume has been in describing the roots of our crisis. In part, as we have seen, it has been brought about because of a philosophical and cultural shift in the western world, from an Enlightenment to a post-Enlightenment perspective, both for ill and for good. People in America and the West seem to be asking different questions and articulating their priorities differently than even 50 years ago. This has certainly been true among Churches of Christ. Because of it, many of our churches are experiencing tension and stress.

A lot of people who grew up in the first half of this century experienced an education system, a set of values, a view of church and country that are quite different from that of children who have grown up more recently. The older generations were required to read more when they were young. In general they are more trusting of institutions and authority. They think with a kind of logic that was perfected during 250 years of western Enlightenment. And, in general, they have a difficult time understanding the values and perspectives of the close-of-the-century generations.

The younger generations tend to be less interested in reading, are more globally aware, have a much less stable view of family and institutions of authority, and are more comfortable with change and variety. Clearly there are countless exceptions to this, but many churches can testify to differences along these lines. Older generations tend to be more interested in content, ideas and doctrines. Younger generations tend to be more interested in experience and in practical ministry and community.

These are not merely generational differences, though they are at least that. It's not inevitable that generations work against each other. But in the cultural and societal shift we are experiencing in the western world, a major fault line seems to separate generations in certain ways creating differences in approach and in priorities. Certainly these differences have helped create the sense for many congregations that the ground is unstable, shaking beneath them.

Partly, the crisis has come about as the sectarian walls that have surrounded us throughout much of this century have begun to topple. Many have peeked over the walls or even climbed over the rubble in a few places, engaging in conversations more broadly with people from other fellowships. This is allowing us both to learn from them as well as influence them. It has become clear that many of the people on the other side of the wall are not barbarians but share many of our values. We are finding it possible to carry on meaningful conversations with people who share common interests and Christian values without relinquishing the teachings to which we are committed.

Similarly, many among us have experienced a crisis of historical consciousness. More and more people have become aware that Churches of Christ have a history, that we did not emerge in the early nineteenth century as the exact replica of the church of the first century, unaffected by the intervening history of Christianity. We understand that our spiritual ancestors on the American frontier, individuals with great ideas and commitments, were nevertheless asking the kinds of questions that people everywhere were asking at the zenith of the Enlightenment, especially in America. And, we discovered, they were reacting to and incorporating many of the teachings and practices of the church in the generations before them. Such awareness in our own day has allowed us to see the human side of religious dialogue and has created a kind of humility that was not so noticeable at the mid-point of the twentieth century.

Moreover, it has become clear that the history of the Restoration Movement is quite complex, that there have always been competing voices, several trajectories of thought. The ones that became the "orthodox" positions of most of our churches in this century are, in some instances, the result of considerable study and hard work but, in other instances, are the result of historical accidents or the influence of powerful preachers. As a people committed to continually re-examining church practices and doctrines in light of Scripture, we should not be surprised that many have actually gone back to the Bible, re-assessed traditional views on a number of issues, and have attempted to change some things in several areas in order to be more faithful to the Word of God as they understand it. Nor should we be surprised that this would cause disagreement, debate, upset, and crisis.

Furthermore, considering the state of American popular culture and its pervasive influence on our lives, it is no surprise that some churches have created programs around utilitarian goals. That is, their overriding question is more about "what works" than ministering out of a strong and healthy biblical theology. If theology is seen primarily as what "academics" do and is, therefore, irrelevant to ordinary Christians, we will find ourselves increasingly diverse as a fellowship for many of the wrong reasons, with some churches careening from fad to fad. The assumption that theology is not practical, that we must simply do whatever it takes to have an effective ministry, certainly feeds the growing pluralism and the sense of crisis within our fellowship.

Similarly, our views on how to study the Bible and how it functions authoritatively for us have undergone significant changes over the last 50 years and this, in turn, has affected the nature and style of our preaching. More and more of our preachers and Bible School teachers, not to mention university professors, are attempting to understand the Bible within its literary, historical, and theological contexts. That is, rather than taking individual verses separate from the overall message and historical occasion, many have attempted to see what problem the text is addressing so that individual verses can be interpreted within the parameters of the original settings.

Those of us who have attempted to understand the Bible in this way often recoil at accusations that such an approach is liberal or that the hermeneutic it employs is new. We believe, in fact, that such an approach is profoundly conservative, that it will keep us from taking human decisions and the conclusions of any generation and giving them the weight and authority of Scripture. It also leads to preaching which is largely expository in nature, viewing each passage in its context and in light of its unfolding theme and message. Listeners who are used to hearing dozens of verses cited from all over the Bible sometimes feel that this approach is not biblical, much to the consternation of the preacher who believes he is walking squarely in the way of the text, trying to say faithfully what Scripture says. This, no doubt, has created a climate of crisis within many Churches of Christ.

Of course, we could add other items to the list of factors precipitating crisis in our churches, issues and practices which often grow out of the interpretive and cultural contexts we have already discussed, most of them having to do with what happens in our worship services. And within individual congregations, these factors combine with the personalities and history of those churches that largely determined how healthy the dialogue among Christians may be.

But while we can describe the crisis in its various forms and suggest possible causes, we do not believe what we are experiencing is unique, either to our fellowship or our day. In fact, as our brief historical survey has indicated, it is not new at all. There has never been a Golden Age. Every generation has seen disputes and change.

Many Christians today, for example, could never imagine a time when Stamps-Baxter music was considered wild, rambunctious, and inappropriate for church. Those who are frustrated at the lack of musical notations on songs displayed on an overhead screen might be surprised that Alexander Campbell himself would be *their* biggest detractor. He argued strongly that musical notes should never be included with the words of our hymns because they detracted from spiritual worship. In ways both large and small, every generation of the church has experienced its share of crises.

We say this partly to urge us not to be overly anxious. While many of the things we are experiencing are not pleasant, and even though the behavior of some of our church leaders is divisive and sinful, we should not see our present crisis with too much alarm. We should, of course, take many matters seriously. Some of the issues really do pertain to our salvation and must be addressed with clarity and urgency. It is possible to hold heretical positions or participate in practices that undermine the cause of Christ. However robust our view of grace may be, it is still possible to be lost. Therefore every Christian should be sober and watchful.

But we must never assume that the future of the church rests on our own shoulders. God is still in charge here. It is his church, not ours. Not only should we go about the business of discipleship with humility and gentleness, we should do so in utter trust in him.

A historian and friend of the Stone-Campbell Movement recently questioned whether or not Churches of Christ will survive in a post-Enlightenment age. He recognizes that the age in which we have lived has deeply affected the questions we have asked, our approach to Scripture and church, and our particular brand of restorationism. For that reason, he rightly asks whether or not the church as we have known it will continue to exist in an era in which this worldview and many of its practices and understandings are dying away.

There are at least a couple of responses to his concerns. First, if in fact our questions and conclusions are utterly time-bound and, therefore, irrelevant for a different day, then perhaps our Movement should die away. If we have nothing relevant to say, we will eventually lose the forum in which to speak.

Many of us believe, however, that the call to restoration ought to bridge the times and transcend the particular methods and eccentricities of a certain era, even the modern one. This would mean, of course, a serious re-thinking of positions and approaches, not to accommodate them to the culture but to approach the Scriptures again in each age, for each generation. It means being part of a church that is adaptive and flexible, allowing the changeless Word to find its voice and its relevance within a changing culture.

Simply from a sociological perspective, if we look at similar circumstances for other groups in other ages, then perhaps these assumptions will not seem so naive. The attempts at restoring the New Testament church during the sixteenth century, through the work of the Reformers, were largely done in a pre-modern–certainly pre-Enlightenment–context. The various groups had to re-think, adjust, and adapt to the onset of a new age, a new way of thinking, but most of them did not die away. Likewise, one should not quickly assume that Churches of Christ, steeped as we have been in Enlightenment thought and methods, will not be able to survive an age in which these approaches will be challenged and perhaps changed.

Second, and more importantly, God is at work in all this. He is sovereign over all our affairs. He will do what he will do. He has chastened people in the past, and he is fully capable of chastening us. He can affect the nations, and he can certainly affect the affairs and future of this fellowship. He calls for us to be faith-ful–to his will, to his Word. He will be faithful in regard to us.

Surely a healthy view of the nature and work of God in our midst will give us a sense of peace and perspective in these troubled times.

Perhaps it would also be helpful to say that many churches, many Christians, will not identify at all with the issues expressed here. Not every church is undergoing an identity crisis. In fact many, perhaps most, churches and Christians are going on about their business in a quite healthy way. They are not in dispute. They worship lovingly and serve faithfully. They are not troubled by every brotherhood rumor, not looking for false teachers behind every rock and stone. They are not swayed by every fad nor are they looking for ways to disassociate themselves from our heritage. They encourage parents to be faithful stewards of their families, people in the workplace to be individuals of integrity, Christians everywhere to be people of character. And they are largely unaffected by the crises which trouble so many of our churches.

If you are in one of those churches, be thankful and work hard to preserve this spirit. But you should be alert. You must not be naive. Disagreements and frustrations are likely, if not inevitable. Every church we know about in the first century had them, and every age since has been marked by them.

But when the disagreements come, let us make sure that we know which issues are worth laying down our lives for and which ones are scuffles best avoided for the sake of the Kingdom. Let us not die at the outer wall when our resources are needed in the capital.

After leaving Hadrian's Wall, our crew made its way to Edinburgh for two days of sightseeing. Doug, always alert for connections with our Christian heritage, arranged for us to visit the old Glasite meeting house there. It was the place of worship for the followers of John Glas whose views had a significant impact on early American restoration leaders.

By the time we had come to Edinburgh, we had seen more Anglican churches, cathedrals, and monasteries than we could count. We had found all of them interesting, though they felt a lot like museums or performance halls to many in the group. But when we entered the Glasite worship house, it was like coming home. It looked very similar to the churches of many of our childhoods–wooden pews, windowless walls, plain pulpit, and prominent communion table. We sat down silently in the front rows and absorbed the occasion and the atmosphere. We began to sing, quietly at first, then with more and more passion and not a few tears.

People from this church a couple of centuries ago had said things, taught things, and done things that had influenced the people who had influenced us. A flood of indebtedness and gratitude filled our hearts and caught in our throats.

But something was missing. The building now belonged to a historical society in Edinburgh. The thriving church of two centuries before had built walls around itself, isolating its members from the religious conversations around them. Those among them who advocated baptism by immersion eventually left. These so-called Scotch Baptists had a great influence both on Baptist Churches in America and people of the Stone-Campbell tradition. The Glasites who remained behind experienced greater and greater retrenchment as their numbers dwindled. They recalled vividly the days of their glory, times in which they were a thriving community of believers within the city of Edinburgh. But those days were now gone. By the time we arrived, the last remaining member of that church had been dead just a few years. The church doors had closed. The dream had died.

Our tears that day were as much for us as for them. In many ways, their dreams were ours, their vision of church and Kingdom were a part of the stream in which we now navigated. How far would we follow them? Would we end up as they did? Would we wall ourselves off from fellow seekers who might give us a new and better vision of Christ and who might gain from the insights we offer? Would we surround ourselves in self-protection only to find ourselves suffocating in self-absorption? Would we wage our most substantial battles at the margins, fussing over matters far removed from the cross of Christ? And would we, in so doing, lose the war at the center?

We pray today for God's help in these things. None of us is wise enough to figure it all out or good enough to do it all right. This is a time to tone down the rhetoric, to listen, to study, to pray, to serve, to let God do the working. This is certainly no time for crowing and posturing, vacillating or compromising. Rather, it is a time for humble surrender, bold proclamation, and quiet service.

Above all, it is a time for hope and confidence, for surely God "doth undertake to guide the future as he has the past."

Bibliography

The authors recommend the following books and articles for further reading. Though we do not fully endorse everything they say, we have found them to be stimulating and useful conversation partners in some of the key areas under consideration in this book.

Tradition & History

Allen, C. Leonard. *Distant Voices: Discovering a Forgotten Past for a Changing Church.* Abilene: ACU Press, 1993.

Allen looks back into the early heritage of the Restoration Movement to identify various currents of thought that became lost or marginalized in the Movement's later years. His premise is that the often neglected early diversity of the Movement can provide help in these days of increasing diversity. One chapter explores the Movement's attitudes towards tradition, in particular the contributions of Burke Aaron Hinsdale.

Barzun, Jacques. *From Dawn to Decadence: 500 Years of Western Cultural Life.* New York: HarperCollins, 2000.

One of the premier historians of the twentieth century writes a lively and often brilliant survey of Western culture. This work is both expansive and readable–a rare combination. This work is no mundane history, no mere recounting of facts and events. Rather Barzun, who has lived almost one hundred of the five hundred years he traces, weaves an engaging and complex tale of philosophy, politics, art, language, religion, and the significant and sometimes forgotten figures of the period. He traces several recurring themes, such as primitivism, individualism, self-consciousness, abstraction, and emancipation, which fueled the rise of the modern era and have contributed to its fall.

Christian Studies is the Journal of the Institute for Christian Studies in Austin. The following two articles are in the 1991 volume dedicated to the subject of tradition in Churches of Christ:

Holloway, Gary N. "Both Catholic and Protestant: Alexander Campbell and Tradition." *Christian Studies* 11:2 (1991) 31-40.

Holloway demonstrates that although Campbell was typically suspicious of tradition, he also welcomed its insights when they did not conflict with Scripture. The article illustrates Campbell's reasoned use of church tradition, even ancient creeds, as a potentially helpful repository of wisdom.

Thompson, James W. "What Every Christian Should Know: Tradition in the Early Church." *Christian Studies* 11:2 (1991) 5-14.

Thompson shows that the New Testament uses the term "tradition" in a variety of senses, good and bad. In particular, he focuses on Paul's use of the term and on the crucial role tradition played in his ministry and in the first-century church. The New Testament does not distinguish between tradition and God's will, but between tradition that furthers God's will and that which subverts it.

Garrett, Leroy. *The Stone-Campbell Movement: The Story of the American Restoration Movement*. Revised edition. Joplin, Missouri: College Press Publishing Company, Inc., 1995.

The best one-volume telling of the story of the Stone-Campbell Restoration Movement available. In his lively narrative style, Garrett examines the people, ideas, and events of the Movement worldwide, focusing on the quest for unity among Christians that has been a key component since the beginning.

Gonzalez, Justo L. *The Story of Christianity: The Early Church to the Dawn of the Reformation,* Volume 1; *The Story of Christianity: Reformation to the Present Day,* Volume 2. San Francisco: Harper San Francisco, 1984,1985.

A fascinating telling of the history of Christianity by an excellent writer and teacher. Gonzalez weaves together the stories of the people, ideas and events that have shaped the church from its beginning to the present in an interesting and often exciting narrative. He describes developments in the church and the connections between believers through the twenty centuries of its existence.

Grenz, Stanley J. *A Primer on Postmodernism.* Grand Rapids: Eerdmans, 1996.

Those interested in an accessible introduction to the cultural and intellectual currents of postmodernism would be well advised to consult this book. Written by a person of faith, this work provides a critical analysis of postmodern trends, its antecedents, its obstacles to the Christian faith, and the opportunities it may provide for presenting and hearing the Gospel in this changing climate.

Hughes, Richard T. *Reviving the Ancient Faith: The Story of Churches of Christ in America.* Grand Rapids: William B. Eerdmans Publishing Company, 1996.

The first true critical history of Churches of Christ, this volume is a must read for anyone wanting to understand how Churches of Christ have been shaped in the last two hundred years. Filled with illustrations and with fascinating and often little-known stories of our heritage, the book is guaranteed to provoke thought and growth.

Williams, D.H. *Retrieving the Tradition and Renewing Evangelicalism: A Primer for Suspicious Protestants.* Grand Rapids: Eerdmans, 1999.

Williams surveys the growth of tradition over the centuries and the changing roles it has had in different churches. He describes the legitimate concerns Protestants have had about relying on church tradition as a religious authority, highlighting the attitudes of Restoration leader Alexander Campbell. Yet he insists that the careful handling of tradition is one of the most deeply needed disciplines in churches today, since silencing the voice of tradition opens the way for illegitimate voices to take over.

Willimon, William H. *Word, Water, Wine, and Bread.* Valley Forge, PA.: Judson Press, 1980.

One of America's foremost Christian writers and thinkers provides a brief survey of the history of Christian worship. Too short for substantial depth or nuance, this work provides a simple and useful overview of major developments in Christian worship and its interconnectedness with Christian history and tradition.

Interpreting Scripture

Fee, Gordon D. and Douglas Stuart. *How to Read the Bible for All its Worth*. 2nd edition. Grand Rapids: Zondervan, 1993.

Aimed at the layperson wanting to study the Bible on their own, this handy introduction to Bible reading focuses on the need to respect the literary qualities of Scripture. In particular, the authors explain the various genres one finds in Scripture, also stressing the need to let context guide one's reading. A systematic presentation that is easy to read, amply illustrated from Bible text.

Malherbe, Abraham. "A People under the Word." *Mission* 1 (1967): 16-20.

Insisting that the Word of God is essentially the message of Christ, Malherbe argues against a view of Scripture that reduces it to a mere blueprint for reconstructing the first-century church, or to a collection of propositions to be mastered. Such views obscure Scripture's function as the manifold and even mysterious revelation of Christ and threaten to handicap Bible interpretation in Churches of Christ.

Middleton, Richard J. and Brian J. Walsh. *Truth is Stranger Than It Used to Be: A Biblical Faith in a Postmodern Age.* Downers Grove: IVP, 1995.

The authors convey a deep respect for the Bible as well as a keen understanding of the changing cultural landscape. They assess the impact of postmodernism on the interpretation of Scripture and provide a responsible way of respecting biblical authority while confronting the challenges and opportunities of this new era.

Olbricht, Thomas H. *Hearing God's Voice: My Life with Scripture in the Churches of Christ*. Abilene: ACU Press, 1996.

This autobiography chronicles the author's lifelong voyage of faith within his Church of Christ heritage. In the light of changing attitudes in the Movement during the twentieth century, the author focuses on the experiences of his life that have had formative impact on his methods of theological reflection and his perspectives on Scripture. The engaging narrative presentation confronts the reader with the inescapable interconnections between hermeneutics, culture, personal experience, and one's community of faith.

Formulating Doctrine

Harris, Randall J. and Rubel Shelly. *The Second Incarnation: A Theology for the 21st-Century Church.* West Monroe, LA: Howard Publishing, 1992.

The authors attempt to do the sort of thing the present book advocates, formulating doctrine in a way that privileges the core teachings of Scripture, the centrality of Christ in particular. The authors insist that constant renewal of doctrine is necessary, both because of human limitations and changing circumstances. Focusing on the specific doctrine of the church, they attempt to formulate an over-arching vision for the church based on Christ, emphasizing the inter-relatedness of Scripture, community, tradition, individuality, ethics, ministry, worship, etc.

Jones, W. Paul. *Theological Worlds. Understanding the Alternative Rhythms of Christian Belief.* Nashville:Abingdon, 1989.

Jones surveys various groups, developing a typology of five common Christian perspectives. Each group tends to be dominated by one of these perspectives, often as a result of their history and circumstances. These perspectives profoundly shape the group's attitudes towards the meaning of the Gospel, the Christian life, and the church. Each supplies important needs, having roots in Scripture and in the broad Christian heritage. By using Jones' typology, Christians can think through the strengths and weaknesses of their own heritage, better understand other perspectives, and perhaps get a grip on the confusion that occurs in a group when the circumstances shaping their perspective changes radically so that they experience an identity crisis.

Stone, Howard W. and James O. Duke. *How To Think Theologically.* Minneapolis: Fortress, 1996.

The authors argue that all Christians are theologians. But in order to make healthy decisions regarding faith and practice, Christians and churches need to engage deliberately in conversations with Scripture and tradition, openly recognizing the roles that human reason and experience necessarily play. Emphasizing the importance of knowing one's own particular biases, the authors challenge Christians to relate all their beliefs and practices to the main topics of Christian doctrine, both individually and communally.

Webber, Robert E. *Ancient-Future Faith. Rethinking Evangelicalism for a Postmodern World.* Grand Rapids: Baker Books, 1999.

The author discusses some of the challenges Christianity presently faces because of recent postmodern shifts, arguing that the church's best opportunity to witness faithfully in a postmodern climate requires a restoration of the essential faith of the first few centuries, with Scripture as the control and foundation. In the areas of Christ, church, worship, spirituality, and mission, the author surveys some problems we have inherited from the Enlightenment in each area, suggesting an angle of approach in each that can bear fruit in a postmodern setting. The book emphasizes authenticity, preaching Christ as the victor over evil, the importance of community rather than individualism, and the powerful meaning of Christian ritual, especially baptism and the Lord's Supper.

Wells, David. *No Place for Truth: Or Whatever Happened to Evangelical Theology?* Grand Rapids: Eerdmans, 1993.

Wells presents a searing critique of conservative Christianity and its inability to address effectively the challenges of this age. A conservative himself, he particularly notes the general lack of interest in marshalling the theological resources needed to face the present cultural circumstances. Without it, he suggests, this intellectual tradition may not survive in the next millennium.

Corinthian Correspondence

Brown, Alexandra R. *The Cross and Human Transformation: Paul's Apocalyptic Word in 1 Corinthians.* Minneapolis: Fortress, 1995.

While many authors have pointed to the cross as a unifying theme in 1 Corinthians, few have done so as powerfully or persuasively as Alexandra Brown. She argues that Paul's message of the cross originated in his apocalyptic understanding, that his readers were in "the ripeness of time" and therefore were called upon to reconcile their differences by the power of the cross. Some will probably find the book somewhat technical, but its thesis and conclusions are compelling.

Fee, Gordon D. *The First Epistle to the Corinthians.* The New International Commentary on the New Testament. Grand Rapids: Eerdmans, 1987.

Fee's introduction to 1 Corinthians provides a vivid description of the problems and concerns Paul faced in writing this epistle. His discussion of the situation at Corinth is quite helpful in framing the issues that have become so familiar to modern readers but often misunderstood. Fee's charismatic tendencies are apparent in his discussion of chapters 12-14, but in general this is a valuable commentary on an important epistle.